# LEGAL PATH SERIES™

# MBE BAR REVIEW

## Multistate Bar Examination (MBE) Review

# LEGAL PATH SERIES™

# MULTISTATE BAR EXAMINATION (MBE) REVIEW

### First Edition

## Peter R. Errico, Esq.
### New York Law School

## Mclaren Legal Publishers LLC
### New York

ISBN 0-9762845-9-6
Library of Congress Control Number: 2004116693

Published by
Mclaren Legal Publishers LLC
136 West 21 Street, 8th Floor
New York, NY 10011

www.mclarenpublishing.com
email: contact@mclarenpublishing.com

**Printed in the United States of America**

# HOW TO USE THIS BOOK

This Multistate Bar Review (MBE) study aid is designed to cover, in both content and format, all of the subject areas tested on the MBE section of the Bar examination.

## "All of what you need, none of what you don't"

This Bar review book was designed to focus, with great precision, on the most commonly tested areas within each of the seven subjects tested. In our experience, roughly 40% – 50% of all the questions on the MBE section of the Bar exam are repeated in some way shape or form year after year. Consequently, the material covered in this book reflects that assumption, but is not restricted by it. Our law school study guide gives you exactly what you need to understand the key principles of each subject area, including the black Letter law and any relevant exceptions. We are not a replacement for an in depth legal analysis of the subject matter covered; however, we do present what is absolutely critical in a very concise format.

## "Look for the Ψ symbol"

We use the Greek capital letter PSI ( **Ψ** ) to indicate a commonly tested and important issue. These topics indicated are the most frequently tested areas on the MBE section of the Bar Examination. Please pay special attention to the subject matter indicated.

# Abbreviations used in this book

(D)................................................................................Defendant

(P)..................................................................................Plaintiff

§ ...............................................................Symbol for "section"

FRCP......................................Federal Rules of Criminal Procedure

NIED...........................Negligent Infliction of Emotional Distress

IIED...........................Intentional Infliction of Emotional Distress

UCC.......................................................Uniform Commercial Code

Ψ............................ Exam Tip symbol (a topic frequently tested)

# TABLE OF CONTENTS

# TORTS

I.    **INTENTIONAL TORTS AGAINST A PERSON**

A.  **Battery**

   1.  One is liable for battery if:
       a.  **He commits a harmful or offensive contact ...**
           - The test for a harmful or offensive contact is what the average person would consider an unpermitted contact.

       b.  **...with the person of another.**
           - The "person of another" element includes anything the person is holding, touching, or connected to.

   2.  One is not liable for the tort of battery if the harmful or offensive contact is committed without intent. Therefore, if the harmful or offensive contact is due to negligence or recklessness, one could not be liable for the tort of battery.

   3.  To commit a battery, the plaintiff does not have to be aware of the harmful or offensive contact. Therefore, if the harmful of offensive contact is committed while one is asleep and unaware of the contact, a tort of battery has still occurred.

B.  **Assault**

   1.  One is liable for *Tortuous* assault if:
       a.  **He causes fear or apprehension of an ...**
           - To recover for assault one must feel reasonable apprehension. Unlike battery, one <u>must have knowledge of the act</u> that causes fear or apprehension.

1

**b. ...immediate battery**

- <u>Words alone are insufficient</u> to commit the tort of assault. However, words could negate the immediacy of the contact. For example, if "A" said to "B," "If you were not my friend, I would hit you." The immediacy of the contact is negated by the conditional statement.

**2. Unloaded Gun Theory**
If the defendant holds a gun to the head of the plaintiff and the plaintiff knows the gun is not loaded, there is no fear or apprehension and thus no assault. However, if plaintiff does not know that the gun lacks ammunition and he is reasonably fearful of a battery, there is an assault.

## C. False Imprisonment Ψ

1. One is liable for false imprisonment if he:
   **a. Commits an act of restraint or confinement**
   ...

   **b. ...of another within a bounded area.**
2. Confinement results when there is physical restraint, threats of force, an institution of barriers that restrain freedom, or providing one with no means of escape.

3. **The Shopkeeper's Privilege**
   There is no tort of false imprisonment against a shopkeeper who detains a suspect for shoplifting if there are: (1) reasonable grounds for the detention; (2) the detention is conducted in a reasonable manner; and (3) the detention is limited to a reasonable period of time.

## D. Intentional Infliction of Emotional Distress (IIED)

One is liable for intentional infliction of emotional distress if:

a.  **He engages in outrageous behavior…**

- Outrageous behavior is defined as conduct that exceeds all bounds of decency tolerated in a civilized society.
- Mere insults are not outrageous.
- Outrageous conduct is conduct that is:

    i.    Continuous or repetitive;

    ii.    Done by a defendant who is a common carrier or innkeeper;

    iii.    Against a fragile class of persons (young children, the elderly, pregnant women); or

    iv.    The result of playing on the known sensitivity of another.

b.  **…which results in another person suffering severe emotional distress.**

- Although physical injuries are not required, the plaintiff must prove actual damages.

**E. Negligent Infliction of Emotional Distress (NIED)**

1. In order to successfully sue for negligent infliction of emotional distress one must prove:

a.  **He was in the zone of danger and threatened with injury by the defendant's negligence; and**

b.  **Endured subsequent physical manifestations due to the negligence of the defendant (heart attack, miscarriage, skin inflammation, or a nervous tick).**

- If the mental harm is not immediate but follows later as a result of the defendant's negligence, courts will not allow recovery for the purely mental elements of the damage.

**F. By-Standard Cases (recovery for grief) Ψ**

1.  In order to recover for grief:
    a.  **Plaintiff must witness the negligent bodily injury; and**

    b.  **The injured party must be a close relative; and**
        • Courts have defined close relatives as spouses, children, parents or siblings.

    c.  **Plaintiff must be in the zone of danger and threatened by the defendant's actions.**

**II.   INTENTIONAL TORTS ON PROPERTY**

**A. Trespass to Land**

1.  One has committed trespass to land if there is a:

    a.  **Physical invasion of; or**

    b.  **Remaining on; or**

    c.  **Fails to remove a thing which he has a duty to remove on the...**

    d.  **land of another**
        The plaintiff that brings an action for trespass to land must have standing. In other words, the plaintiff must be in either actual possession of the land in question or have the right of possession.

2.  Intent to enter onto the land is sufficient for a trespass to land. It is no defense that there was a mistake as to ownership.

3.  In addition to a trespass being committed on one's land, a trespass could be committed above or

beneath the surface of the land. Therefore, one is not permitted to dig tunnels under another's land nor could one allow a tree to hang over the property of another.

**4. Privileged Trespasses**
A party is privileged to trespass onto the land of another if for a "public" or "private" necessity. In such situations, the defendant is liable only for damage to the land but not for trespass.

**5. Accidental Trespasses**
There is no liability for an accidental trespass if it is non-negligent and unintentional.

**6. Negligent or Reckless Trespasses**
One who negligently or recklessly enters the land of another and causes damage is liable for the damage to the land. If there is no damage, then the plaintiff could recover only nominal damages.

**B. Trespass to Chattels**

One has committed trespass to chattels if there is a:

**a. Deliberate interference with personal property; and**
- Plaintiff must own property; and
- The (D) must initially interfere with the possession of that property.

**b. Damages**
- The (P) must prove either the dollar amount in damages caused by the tort or the value due to the loss of the use of the chattel.
- Mistake of ownership of the chattel is no defense to trespass to chattels.

## C. Conversion

1. One has committed a conversion if there is a:
   **a. Deliberate exercise of dominion or control over the personal property of another...**

   - Plaintiff must own property or be in rightful possession of it.
   - Only personal property can be converted. Real property cannot be converted but could be adversely possessed.

   **b. ...which seriously interferes with the owner's right to control it.**

   - Plaintiff is entitled to the full value of the object at the time of the conversion.
   - Mistake of ownership of the chattel is no defense to conversion.

2. Comparing and Contrasting Trespass to Chattels and Conversion Ψ

| Trespass to Chattels | Conversion |
|---|---|
| Intentional tort | Intentional tort |
| Interference with the chattel of another. | Exercising dominion or control over the chattel of another. |
| Defendant is liable for damages to the chattel. | Defendant is liable for the replacement of the chattel. |

## III. AFFIRMATIVE DEFENSES TO INTENTIONAL TORTS Ψ

### A. Consent

1. Consent requires the defendant to demonstrate the legal capacity of the plaintiff's willingness to have the defendant invade his interests. Consent could be either express or implied.

**TORTS**      LEGAL PATH
MULTISTATE BAR EXAMINATION
REVIEW      **TORTS**

2.   Express Consent is a defense to an intentional tort when made by the plaintiff to the defendant. For example, if a patient expressly consents to a surgical procedure, the surgeon has a defense of consent to the patient's battery claim.

3.   Implied Consent is a defense to intentional torts when it is implied by law or apparent from the plaintiff's conduct.

- Implied consent could arise from custom or usage. For example, if one is pushed by another when a subway car comes to an abrupt stop, there is an implied consent due to custom. Furthermore, there is implied consent when playing some sports that require physical contact due to the nature of the sport.

**B. Self-defense**

1.   One may use reasonable force, not intended or likely to cause death or serious bodily harm, in defending oneself against non-consensual harmful or offensive contact.

2.   One is only permitted to use force if the threat is immediate or in progress. If the threat has ended, no privilege exists.

3.   One must have a reasonable belief that the threat is genuine in order to allege self-defense.

- An honest and good faith reasonable mistake will not deny one the use of one of the privileges, which is usually determined by a jury.

4.   One must limit one's self to the appropriate force.

- Whatever force is necessary under the circumstances is allowable.

- Deadly force could be used if human life is endangered, but is never allowed to protect property.

## C. Defense of Others

1.  One is privileged to defend others from a harmful or offensive contact under the same principles as a defense of oneself if:
    a.  The circumstances warrant the defense of another; and
    b.  The defense of the other is necessary for the protection of that person.

## D. Defense of Property

1.  One is privileged to use reasonable force, not intended or likely to cause death or serious bodily harm, to prevent intrusion or destruction of property.

2.  One may never use force that is capable of causing death or serious bodily harm to defend property unless there is a threat to one's own safety that justifies the use of such force.

## E. Necessity

1.  Necessity is a defense that is only available in property torts.

2.  **Public Necessity**
    A public necessity is where a defendant interferes with (P's) property in an emergency situation in order to protect the community.

    - If the defendant reasonably believes that the interference with the plaintiff's land is necessary, he will be privileged to do so. Even if the interference is not necessary, but the defendant reasonably believes that it is, the entry will be privileged.

- Public necessity is an absolute defense and the defendant is not liable for trespass or damage to the property or chattel.

3.  **Private Necessity**
    A private necessity is when a defendant interferes with (P's) property in an emergency situation in order to protect his own interest.

    - This is not an absolute defense. The defendant is not liable for the trespass but is liable for the damages caused.
    - However, the defendant is not liable for nominal or punitive damages.
    - As long as the emergency continues, the defendant cannot be expelled from or forced off the land by the plaintiff.

F.  **Privilege**

    1.  Privileges exist where there is:
        a.  Consent by the plaintiff; or
        b.  An important public interest to be protected by the defendant's normally prohibited behavior.
    2.  The defendant has the burden of proof to prove the existence of the privilege and that he acted reasonably under the circumstances.

IV.  **DEFAMATION**

A.  **Comparing and Contrasting Libel and Slander**

    1.  Libel is the publication of a defamatory statement, which is written or printed.
    2.  Slander is the publication of a defamatory statement which is spoken.

## B. The Elements of Defamation Ψ

1. **Defamatory statement against the plaintiff**
   a. A defamatory statement is a statement that is "of and concerning" the plaintiff which subjects him to ridicule by other members of the community.

   b. The court determines if the statement was defamatory and the jury determines if the material was understood to be defamatory.

2. **The statement is published**
   a. "Publication" means that the statement was communicated to at least one other person other than the plaintiff.

   b. The person the statement is communicated to has to understand the statement to be defamatory to the plaintiff.

   c. Persons who repeat the defamatory statement are liable to the same extent as the primary publisher.

   d. Each repetition of the defamatory statement is a publication except for repetition by newspapers, magazines and the like, which are considered a single publication.

3. **The plaintiff suffers damages**
   a. There are two types of damages: general and special. The ability to recover on either or both depends on whether the defamation is libel or slander.

b.  The law presumes general damages and the defendant need not prove anything to recover.

c.  Special damages require the plaintiff to prove a pecuniary loss due to the defamation.

d.  Slander requires the proof of special damages unless the statement is *slander per se*. Instances of *slander per se* occur when the statement made states the plaintiff has:

- A loathsome disease;
- Is unchaste;
- Committed a crime of moral turpitude; or
- Reflects on one's profession, business or trade.

e.  Unlike slander, general damages are presumed in libel cases and usually special damages need not be proven to recover.

4.  **Defendant's lack of a defense**
    a.  **Consent**
        If there is consent by the affected party to the publication of the defamatory material, the defendant has a defense.

    b.  **Truth**
        If the defamatory statement is true, the defendant has a defense.

    c.  **Retraction**
        If the retraction is immediate after publication, and is enough to negate the defamatory effect, the retraction will be a defense.

d. **Privilege**

- **Absolute Privilege**
  A defamatory statement is absolutely privileged in the following situations: (1) statements in the course of judicial proceedings or legislative proceedings; (2) statements between a husband and wife; and (3) compelled broadcasts (material which is required to be published by radio, television or newspapers).

- **Conditional Privilege**
  A defamatory statement is conditionally privileged if the statement is made (1) in good faith; (2) based on a reasonable belief; and (3) disclosure is limited to those who can act.

## V. PRIVACY TORTS Ψ

### A. Appropriation of Defendant's Name or Likeness
One is liable for the tort of appropriation if one uses the plaintiff's name and likeness for a commercial advantage.

- A commercial advantage requires the defendant to use the plaintiff's name or likeness in connection with the promotion or advertisement of a product or service.

### B. Intrusion upon Seclusion (and Solitude)
One is liable for the tort of intrusion upon seclusion if the defendant intentionally intrudes upon the plaintiff's seclusion in a way objectionable to the average person.

- There must be an expectation of privacy by the plaintiff for a defendant to be liable for intrusion upon seclusion.
- Examples of intrusion upon seclusion are: wire tapping, eavesdropping and peeping toms.

### C. Placing a Person in a False Light

One is liable for the tort of placing a person in a false light if one widely disseminates a falsehood of the plaintiff that would be objectionable to the average person.

- The tort of placing a person in a false light is usually a tort used when the plaintiff cannot sufficiently prove a defamation claim.
- Placing a person in a false light is not intentional, therefore mistake is no defense.

### D. Disclosure of Private Facts

One is liable for disclosure of private facts if one widely disseminates the confidential information of another that the average person would find objectionable.

- Disclosure of private facts is a tort - except if the disclosure is newsworthy material.
- **Dual Life Doctrine**
  If a person lives two lives, one where information is kept secret and the other where the information is known by others; and if the secret information is spread to persons who were unaware of the hidden life, there exists no tort.

## VI. MISCELLANEOUS TORTS

### A. Fraud

1.  One has committed fraud if all of the following elements are present:

    a.  Affirmative misrepresentation of fact by the defendant;
    b.  Intent to induce the plaintiff to act;
    c.  Causation;
    d.  Plaintiff must justifiably rely on the misrepresentation; and
    e.  Damages result.

2.  One is generally not guilty of fraud for a failure to disclose information. However, there are a few

exceptions to this principle. If there is a fiduciary relationship between the parties there is a requirement to disclose all material facts. In addition, one cannot make incomplete statements that are misleading or actively conceal information.

**B.  Tortuous Interference with a Contract**

1.  One has tortuously interfered with a contract if all of the following elements are present:

    a.  There exists a valid contract, not terminable at will, between plaintiff and a third party;

    b.  The defendant knows of the contract between plaintiff and the third party;

    c.  The defendant causes a third party to abandon or breach the contract between plaintiff and the third party;

    d.  There is an actual breach of the contract; and

    e.  Damages result.

2.  Any type of contract may be a basis for this type of tort action as long as the contract is enforceable, legal and not against public policy.

3.  Damages could be at law or in equity. Where damages have been sustained, an action at law is appropriate. Depending on the court, damages could be limited to those that are foreseeable or those that are proximate. If damages are not an appropriate remedy, a party may seek injunctive (equitable) relief as a remedy.

## C. Nuisance

1. Public vs. Private Nuisance

   a. **Public Nuisance**
      A public nuisance is the unreasonable
      interference with public rights.

      - Types of interference associated with public
        nuisances are interferences with public
        health, safety, peace and comfort.
      - Certain conduct could be a public nuisance
        if it is proscribed by statute, ordinance or
        regulation.
      - A private person could recover for a public
        nuisance if he could prove he suffered a
        harm different from that sustained by the
        public.

   b. **Private Nuisance**
      A private nuisance is the substantial and
      unreasonable interference with the use and
      enjoyment of one's land.
      - A substantial interference is that which is
        offensive or inconvenient to the average
        person.
      - The interference is unreasonable if the
        plaintiff's harm is outweighed by the
        defendant's conduct.

2. Defenses to Nuisance
   a. **Contributory Negligence**
      If the nuisance results from the negligent
      conduct of the defendant, the plaintiff's
      contributory negligence is a defense. However,
      if the defendant's harm is intentional, then
      contributory negligence is not a defense.

   b. **Coming to the Nuisance**
      Coming to the nuisance is where one acquires
      land <u>after</u> the nuisance and then files a nuisance

cause of action. This is not by itself a complete defense, but is a factor to be considered.

3.  Remedies for Nuisance Torts
    **a.  Damages**
    If money damages are appropriate, the affected party may sue for damages.

    **b.  Injunctive Relief**
    If money damages are not an adequate remedy a court may, in its discretion, grant an injunction.

    **c.  Abatement by Self-Help**
    Abatement by self-help is a remedy that allows the (P) to enter upon the defendant's land and personally abate the nuisance. Before abatement is allowed, the plaintiff must give notice to the (D) and he, the (D), must refuse to act. This privilege extends to all reasonable actions which are necessary to terminate the nuisance.

**D.  Malicious Prosecution**

One is subject to liability for malicious prosecution if all of the following elements are found:

a.  The defendant initiates legal proceedings without probable cause. Probable cause is one's reasonable belief that another's actions constitute an offense;

b.  The defendant initiated the procedure for a purpose other than that of bringing the offender to justice; and

c.  The proceedings have terminated in favor of the accused.

### E. Abuse of Process

Abuse of process is the wrongful use of the legal process against another for a purpose for which it is not designed.

### F. Prima Facie Tort

The elements of a prima facie tort are (1) the intentional infliction (2) of pecuniary harm (3) without justification.

## VII. NEGLIGENCE

Negligence is conduct that falls below the standard established by law for the protection of others against an unreasonable risk of harm. Negligent conduct may be either an act which the actor, as a reasonable person, should recognize as involving an unreasonable risk of causing an invasion of the interests of another; or a failure to act which is necessary for the protection or assistance of another and which the actor is under some duty to do.

### A. The Elements of Negligence Ψ

1. **The defendant owes the plaintiff a duty against unreasonable harm.**

   a. There are two issues associated with this element:

   **(1) Who are the members of the class who are owed a duty?**

   - **Majority View**
     The majority view established by Cardozo is the "zone of danger" analysis. The zone of danger is the area that includes all potential victims. Under this theory, anyone within the zone of danger is owed a duty of care.

- **Minority View**
  The minority view established by Andrews states that anyone who suffers an injury as a proximate result of the defendant's breach is owed a duty of care.

**(2) What is the standard of care owed?**

- **Reasonable Person Standard of Care**
  For most negligent actions, an act is negligent only if the actor fails to use reasonable care. Reasonable care is defined as the standard of care that a reasonable person would exercise in the same position under similar circumstances.

- **Standard of Care for Children**
  Children under the age of four are incapable of negligence. For all other children, the standard is that of a child of similar age, experience and intelligence. Children engaged in adult activities (operating a motorized machine with an engine) are held to a reasonable adult standard of care.

- **Standard of Care for Physicians**
  The standard of care for physicians is the same care that is given by the average doctor in a similar community. If a doctor practices in a big city, he is compared to a doctor of a similar big city. Specialists (for example, pediatric surgeons) are held to the standard of care of specialists nationally.

- **Employer/Employee Standard of Care**
  The doctrine that governs the employer-employee standard of care is respondeat

superior. Respondeat superior holds the employer vicariously liable for the active wrongdoing of an employee in the following situations:

i.      An employer is vicariously liable for the torts of its employee who is acting within the scope of his employment.

ii.     An employer is vicariously liable for the torts of his employee who is outside the scope of his employment but is on the employer's premises or is using the chattel of the employer.

iii.    An employer is vicariously liable for the torts of his employee which are intentional.

- **Parents' Standard of Care Owed for their Children's Torts**
  Parents are not liable for the torts of their children.

- **Standard owed by Occupiers of Land**

  **(1) Invitees**
  An invitee is a person who enters the land of another <u>for business</u> involving the occupier and upon his invitation. The standard owed by an occupier of land to an invitee is reasonable care in keeping the property safe and to warn of dangerous conditions the invitee is unlikely to discover.

### (2) Licensees

A licensee is a person who enters the land of another with permission for a purpose that does not benefit the possessor of the land (guest at a party). The standard of care owed by the occupier of land to a licensee is to warn of unknown or dangerous conditions.

### (3) Innkeepers and Common Carriers

Innkeepers are people who run hotels and other overnight living establishments. The standard of care for innkeepers is very high; they are liable for even the slightest negligence.

Common carriers include buses, taxis, trains and planes and also require a high degree of care.

### (4) Trespassers

There is no duty owed to an unknown trespasser. However, a known trespasser is owed a duty of ordinary care to warn and make safe land conditions that involve a risk of death or serious injury.

### Attractive Nuisance Doctrine

The attractive nuisance doctrine applies where a child has trespassed on another's land due to an attractive <u>artificial</u> condition. The elements of an attractive nuisance are:

    i.    The possessor of land knows or should know of the dangerous artificial condition.

    ii.    The possessor of land knows or should know that children play

there and that a dangerous
condition exists that attracts them.

iii. The dangerous condition is likely
to cause an injury to children
because the children are unable to
appreciate the risk.

iv. The cost to protect against the
harm is outweighed by the danger
to the child.

**Duty Comparison Chart Ψ**

| Occupier of Land | Duty Owed |
|---|---|
| Unknown trespasser | No duty owed |
| Known trespasser | Duty to warn and make safe |
| Licensee | Duty to warn |
| Invitee | Duty to warn and inspect premises |
| Innkeepers and common carriers | High degree of care owed |

**(5) Standard Owed by Statute**
Negligence per se refers to the liability
imposed when a statute codifies the duty for
the benefit of a class. Liability for
negligence per se satisfies the elements of
duty and breach but one still has to prove
causation and damages.

The elements of negligence per se are:

a. A statute enacted to prevent the kind of
harm suffered by the plaintiff.
b. The statute defines the standard of care.

c.  The plaintiff is part of the class to be
    protected by the statute.
d.  The statute was created to prevent this type
    of injury.

## 2. Breach of the Duty by the Defendant

A defendant breaches his duty of care if he fails to
conform his conduct to the legally required standard.

### Res Ipsa Liquator

In addition to proving non-conformity to the
standard of care, breach of duty could be
established where the defendant's negligence
could be inferred using circumstantial evidence.
The doctrine is known as *res ipsa liquator*. The
elements the plaintiff must prove to establish *res
ipsa liquator* are:

(1) The injury to the plaintiff was the type that
    does not normally occur absent negligence;
(2) The instrumentality that caused the injury
    was under the exclusive control of the
    defendant; and
(3) The plaintiff is free from contributory
    negligence.

## 3. Causation of the Injury Due to the Breach

This element of negligence asks the question: "Was
there a causal connection, both factually and legally,
between the breach and the injury?"

### a. Factual Causation

Factual causation is the link between the breach
and the injury. There are two types:

- **Direct Factual Causation**
  Direct factual causation is where the injury
  results directly from the breach of the duty
  and there is no other event that contributes

to the plaintiff's injuries. In such a situation, the plaintiff must satisfy the "but-for test". The but-for test is satisfied when "but for the defendant's conduct, the plaintiff would not have been injured".

- **Indirect Factual Causation**
  A defendant is the indirect factual cause of an injury where there is an intervening event in addition to the defendant's breach of duty that causes the resultant injury to the plaintiff. In such a situation, the plaintiff must satisfy the "substantial factor test". If the defendant was a "substantial factor in bringing about the injury to plaintiff" then the test is satisfied.

b. **Legal Causation**
In addition to being a cause in fact of the plaintiff's harm, the defendant's conduct must also be the proximate cause (aka legal cause) of the injury. There are two types:

- **Actual Direct Causation**
  If the defendant is the direct cause of plaintiff's injury and the "but for" test is satisfied, then the defendant is also the legal cause of the injury due to the fact that there is no other event to break the chain of causation.

- **Actual Indirect Causation**
  Actual indirect causation requires a legal cause analysis to determine if the intervening event rises to the level of a superseding event. If the event is superseding, then the chain of causation is broken and the defendant is relieved

of liability. If the event is intervening, then the chain of causation is not broken and the defendant is not relieved of liability.

Intervening acts are those that are foreseeable. Examples of intervening acts that do not cut off the defendant's liability are: intervening medical malpractice, an intervening negligent rescuer or a subsequent disease.

Superseding acts are those that are both unforeseeable and cause an injury different from the one which would have caused the defendant's breach. Examples of superseding acts that cut off the defendant's liability are: third party criminal acts, third party intentional acts, third parties extra ordinary negligence and acts of God.

## 4. Injury to Plaintiff or Plaintiff's Property

a. In order to satisfy this element of negligence, there must be actual harm as a result of physical contact or emotional distress due to the negligent act.

b. A plaintiff may receive punitive damages if it is found that the defendant's action were willful and wanton.

c. **Collateral Source Rule**
Damages are not reduced as a result of benefits received by the plaintiff via other sources (e.g. insurance proceeds).

d. **Eggshell Plaintiff Theory**
The defendant bears the risk that the type of injury will be greater than could be foreseen.

5. **Lack of Defenses**

A defense to negligence will bar the plaintiff's recovery under common law. Some states have deviated from this approach and allowed a recovery where there is a defense. Therefore, before applying a defense, one must look at the law of the jurisdiction in question.

a. **Contributory Negligence Jurisdiction** Ψ
In a contributory negligence jurisdiction, if the plaintiff contributes in any way to his damages, he is fully barred from recovery. The burden of proof is on the plaintiff to show that she is free from fault.

b. **Comparative Negligence Jurisdiction** Ψ
In a comparative negligence jurisdiction, if the plaintiff contributes to his damages, his recovery will be reduced by the percentage of fault the jury assigns to him. There are two types:

- **Pure Comparative Negligence Jurisdiction**
  In a pure comparative negligence jurisdiction, the plaintiff recovers for his damages no matter what percentage of fault the jury assigns to him (even if plaintiff is 95% at fault, he still can recover 5%).

- **Modified Comparative Negligence Jurisdiction**
  In a modified comparative negligence jurisdiction, the plaintiff may not recover any damages if he is more than 50% at fault.

c.   **Assumption of Risk**
A plaintiff who voluntarily assumes the risk of
injury arising from the negligent conduct of the
defendant cannot recover for her injuries.  The
two elements of assumption of risk are that (1)
the plaintiff had knowledge of the risk of harm
and (2) the plaintiff voluntarily assumed the risk.

## VIII.   STRICT LIABILITY CRIMES Ψ
There are three types of conduct where the defendant will be
held strictly liable for the injuries of another despite the
defendant's negligence.

### A.  Injuries by Animals

#### 1. Wild Animals
As long as the plaintiff did nothing to provoke the
wild animal, the owner is strictly liable for the injuries
it causes.

#### 2. Domestic Animals
If the owner has knowledge of a pet's vicious
propensities, he will be strictly liable for the injuries
the animal causes. If the owner has no such
knowledge, then the owner is not strictly liable.

### B.  Ultra-Hazardous Activity
A person who carries out ultra-hazardous activities is strictly
liable for the harm caused to persons, land and chattels
resulting from that activity.  In determining what is
considered an ultra-hazardous activity, a majority of courts
consider the following factors: (1) the activity poses a risk of
serious harm to others or property; (2) the activity cannot be
performed without the risk of serious harm, irrespective of
the amount of care exercised; and (3) the activity is not one
commonly engaged in by persons of the community.  If such
an activity satisfies the above three factors, it is considered

ultra-hazardous and the defendant will be held strictly liable for the injuries the activity may cause.

## C. Strict Liability for Products

There are many theories of liability a plaintiff may use when a product is defective. They are: negligence, implied warranty of merchantability and implied warranty for a particular purpose. However, the emphasis in this section is on strict liability.

The elements 1 – 5 listed below for the strict liability of products are similar to those of negligence and are as follows:

1. The defendant is a manufacturer or supplier engaged in the business of selling the product in question.

   - A manufacturer is defined as anyone who assembles the product or is a retailer or wholesaler of the product.
   - A supplier of a product is defined as anyone who is directly or indirectly associated with the manufacturing of the product.

2. There is a duty by the defendant to make a safe product.

3. The defendant breached his duty due to the fact that the product was unreasonably dangerous or defective.

   - A defendant may breach his duty by producing a product with a manufacturing defect, design defect or not affixing a proper warning on the product. A manufacturing defect is evident where a product was produced in a manner which deviated from its original manufacturing specification. A design defect is evident in a line of identical products each of which have the same dangerous propensities.

4.  The defect exists while in the hands of the defendant.

5.  Actual harm has been caused to a person(s) or to property.

    *   Plaintiff must establish causation of his injury by establishing factual causation and legal causation discussed above.

## D. Defenses to Strict Liability

1.  Comparative fault principles (discussed above).
2.  Assumption of risk (discussed above).
3.  Consumer misuse of product.
4.  Consumer failure to follow directions.
5.  Consumer's failure to heed warnings of the product.

# EVIDENCE

## I. RELEVANCY

### A. Relevant Evidence Definition
Relevant evidence is evidence having the tendency to make a material fact more or less probable then it would be without the evidence.

### B. Exclusion of Relevant Evidence Ψ
Relevant evidence is excluded when its probative value is substantially outweighed by its prejudicial effect due to:
1. Unfair prejudice.
2. Excessive volume.
3. Undue delay.
4. Confusion of issues that may mislead the jury.
5. Waste of time.
6. Cumulative evidence (two witnesses could testify effectively whereas 20 would not be necessary).

### C. Similar Occurrences
In general, if evidence concerns the same time, event or person other than the evidence involved in the case at hand, that evidence is inadmissible.

   a. The following similar occurrences are admissible:

- **Evidence of an Accident History**
  Evidence of ones accident history is inadmissible <u>except</u> to prove:

  1. A fraudulent scheme or plan; or
  2. Defendant's damages were caused by a previous accident not related to the accident at hand.

- **Evidence of a Similar Accident**
  Evidence of a similar accident is generally inadmissible. However, if the accident is caused

by the same instrumentality or condition and occurred under the same or substantially similar circumstances (to show the existence of a dangerous condition), the evidence may be admitted to prove prior notice to the defendant.

An absence of a similar accident may be proven if the accident is caused by the same instrumentality or condition and occurred under the same or substantially similar circumstances.

- **Experiments**
  Experiments are admissible under the same or substantially similar circumstances in order to draw an inference.

- **Comparable Sales**
  Comparable sales are admissible to prove similar sales if there is a substantial similarity of circumstances.

- **Industry Custom**
  Evidence of industry custom may be admitted as evidence to show the appropriate standard of care

- **Habit**
  Habit evidence is admissible to show how the person acted on the occasion at issue. In order for habit evidence to be admissible, there must be both frequency of the conduct and specificity of the conduct.

## D. Public Policy Exclusions of Relevant Evidence

Although some evidence is relevant, it may be excluded due to public policy considerations. The following relevant types of evidence are excluded for public policy reasons:

1. **Subsequent Remedial Measures**
   Subsequent remedial measures are inadmissible to prove negligence, culpability, a defect or a need for a warning. However, subsequent remedial measures are admissible to dispute or prove ownership, control or to show that precautionary measures were possible.

2. **Settlement Offers Ψ**

   a. **Civil Cases**
      - Settlement offers in civil cases are inadmissible to prove liability. Admissions made in connection with settlement offers are also inadmissible; except to impeach, to establish bias, controvert a contention of undue delay by one of the parties or show an attempt to obstruct a criminal investigation.

   b. **Criminal Cases**
      Settlement offers cannot be used against a defendant. Settlement offers include offers to plead guilty, the withdrawal of guilty plea or pleas of no contest. However, in cases of perjury, prosecutions or impeachment, settlement offers may be admissible. Statements made in connection with offers to settle are also inadmissible.

3. **Offers to Pay Medical or Similar Expenses**
   Offers to pay medical or similar expenses are inadmissible to prove a defendant's liability for the plaintiff's injury. Admissions coupled with an offer to pay may be severed and may be admissible.

4. **Liability Insurance**
   Evidence that one did or did not have insurance is inadmissible to prove the defendant was negligent or

that the defendant has the ability to pay a substantial judgment. However, proof of liability insurance is admissible for impeachment purposes, to prove an agency relationship between a witness and the defendant or to show ownership, control or the bias of the witness.

## II.    CHARACTER EVIDENCE Ψ

Character evidence, which is evidence of a person's character or a trait of character, is inadmissible for the purposes of proving action in conformity therewith on a particular occasion. However, the following are <u>exceptions</u> where character evidence is admissible:

### A.  Criminal Cases

A defendant in a criminal case could use evidence of character in the following ways:

1.  Evidence of defendant's character is not admissible in the prosecution's case-in-chief except if the defendant raises the defense of entrapment or the prosecutor wants to prove the defendant was the first aggressor in a homicide case.

2.  **Defendant could "Open the Door"**
    If defendant offers evidence of his good character by reputation or opinion evidence, the prosecution may rebut (introduce character evidence). However, the introduced character trait has to relate to the charge. Rebuttal is limited to reputation and opinion evidence, but the prosecution could ask, "Have you heard" or "Did you know" questions of specific acts about the (D).

3. **Bad character of the victim**

The defense may use reputation, opinion or specific acts to prove the bad character of the victim and the prosecution may so rebut. However, the prosecution could offer evidence of the victim's good character as well as the defendant's character for violence.

6. **Sexual Assault Cases**

Reputation and opinion evidence are inadmissible against the defendant in sexual assault cases but specific acts of sexual behavior by the victim are admissible in the following circumstances:

- To protect the (D's) constitutional rights.
- To prove the victim consented.
- To prove that a person, other that the defendant, is the source of the semen, injuries or other physical evidence of the sexual assault.

B. **Civil Cases**

Character evidence in civil cases is usually inadmissible to prove conduct in conformity with the character. However, character evidence is admissible and could be proven by reputation, opinion or specific acts, in cases where character is an essential element of the claim or defense. Examples of such cases are negligent hiring, defamation or child custody.

C. **Criminal or Civil Cases**

1. **MIMIC PO**

Past conduct is admissible against a (D) to illustrate or establish an element of a present crime. Past conduct is admissible to prove the (D's):

- (M)otive
- (I)ntent
- (M)istake, Lack of
- (I)dentity
- (C)ommon Plan or Scheme

- (P)reparation
- (O)pportunity.

Such evidence may not be offered in the prosecution's case-in-chief but may be offered in rebuttal if the specific trait to be proven is at issue. However, the admissibility of such evidence is subject to the exclusionary rule if its probative value is outweighed by its prejudicial effect.

2. **Sexual Misconduct**
   In a case alleging sexual assault or child molestation, prior specific sexual misconduct of the defendant is admissible as part of the prosecution's case-in-chief or for any relevant purpose including the defendant's propensity to commit the crime.

## III. AUTHENTICATION OF WRITINGS

All evidence, whether it is direct or circumstantial, is classified into three categories: real evidence, demonstrative evidence or scientific evidence. Real evidence includes documentary evidence, tangible objects, or voice samples. Demonstrative evidence is evidence whose relevancy depends on its ability to explain or duplicate material facts. Demonstrative evidence includes models, maps and charts. Scientific evidence includes forensic or ballistic evidence, blood tests or any chemical analysis. Authentication of scientific tests requires that: (1) the device be in proper working condition; (2) the device be operated by a qualified individual; and (3) the technique is one which is generally accepted in the scientific field.

### A. Authentication of Writings

After the relevancy of a writing, which is broadly defined, is determined, it must be authenticated before it is admitted into evidence. Authentication is the laying of a foundation for the evidence to allow a finding of what the evidence purports to be.

- Proof of one's handwriting could be established by: a lay person who is familiar with or has a routine exposure to the handwriting, by expert testimony or by a jury comparison.

**B. Authentication of Objects**
Personal objects could be authenticated by the testimony of one with personal knowledge of it, via distinctive markings or by chain of custody.

**C. Ancient Documents Rule**
The "ancient documents rule" allows a document to be authenticated by evidence that:

- It is at least twenty years old (Federal Rules) or thirty years old (common law);
- Is in such a condition as to be free from suspicion concerning its authenticity; and
- Found in a place where such writings would likely be kept.

**D. Self-authenticating Documents**
There are certain documents that are self-proving and require no authentication. The following are examples of self-authenticating documents: official publications, certified copies of public records, material in newspapers or magazines, documents accompanied by a certificate or authentication, commercial paper and trade inscriptions on business materials.

**E. The Best Evidence Rule**
The "best evidence rule" requires the original writing to be offered into evidence where the writing is material to the case at hand. If there is no original, then copies or oral testimony is admissible after it is proven the original is unavailable.

- Duplicates, which are exact copies of the original produced by the same impression as the original, are admissible as originals in federal court unless the authenticity is challenged or it would be unfair to admit the duplicate in place of the original.

- The best evidence rule applies to the following writings:
  1. Legally Operative Documents – deeds, mortgages, divorce decrees, and contracts.
  2. Writing Offered to Prove an Event – receipts to prove payment, x-rays to prove injuries.
  3. Where the Testimony is Reliant on the Writing, Not on Personal Knowledge – personal knowledge is admissible but writing requires the original document.

- The best evidence rule does not apply:
  1. Merely to prove the writing existed or that a statement was made.
  2. Where facts to be proven exist independently of any legally operative writing (coincidence).
  3. Where evidence collateral to the litigated issue exists.

## IV.    WITNESSES

### A. Competency of Witnesses

Witnesses are presumed to be competent if they have personal knowledge, take an oath or affirmation to testify truthfully and they are sworn in. Even a drunken witness may be competent to testify at trial, if the above criteria are met, although he is still open to cross-examination by the opposing party.

## Specific Requirements for Competent Witnesses Ψ

| Judge as Witness | A presiding judge is disqualified as a witness |
|---|---|
| Attorneys as Witnesses | Attorneys could be witnesses if they are competent but are subject to ethical standards. |
| Jurors as Witnesses | Jurors are disqualified as witnesses in cases where they sit presently as jurors and either the defense or the prosecution objects. |

### B. The Dead Man's Statute

Under the Federal Rules of Evidence, a witness is generally not incompetent to testify merely because he has an interest in the outcome of the litigation. However, some states have enacted Dead Man's Statutes. The Dead Man's Statute states that a party could not testify about personal communications or specific transactions against the estate of a dead person if he has an interest in the outcome of the litigation. The purpose of this rule is to prevent unfairness against the decedent and avoid the possibility of perjury if the witness has a financial interest in the outcome of the descendant's estate and/or distribution of a money judgment. Such claims are not refutable since the decedent cannot speak for himself on the stand. Exceptions to the Dead Man's Statute include: (1) testifying as to what happened after the death of the deceased and (2) where the representative of the estate "opens the door." The estate representative could "open the door" in the following ways:

1. If the protected party calls the interested party to testify.

2. If the testimony of the deceased is given at a prior proceeding or deposition and is read into

evidence, the interested part could explain the matter.

3. If an agent of the deceased testifies as to a transaction with the interested party, the interested party could testify as to the same transaction.

4. If the representative of the deceased fails to make a timely objection.

## C. Impeachment of Witnesses

Generally, impeachment is the casting of an adverse reflection on the veracity of a witness. A witness's credibility cannot be bolstered if his credibility is not attacked. Impeachment is generally used on cross-examination and not on direct testimony. Any matter that tends to prove or disprove the credibility of a witness is relevant for impeachment purposes. Additionally, evidence that is introduced for impeachment purposes is exempt from the hearsay rule because the evidence is not hearsay. Hearsay evidence is evidence introduced for its truth, whereas impeachment evidence is being introduced for impeachment purposes. Under the common law, one may not impeach one's own witness, whereas under the Federal Rules of Evidence one can impeach one's own witness.

## D. Methods of impeachment Ψ

The following are ways a witness could be shown not to be credible:

### 1. Prior Inconsistent Statements

Prior inconsistent statements are those statements made by a party at some other time that conflict or are inconsistent with a material part of his testimony. A prior inconsistent statement cannot be used as substantive evidence except those prior inconsistent statements given orally, under oath and as part of a formal proceeding. Statements made in violation of one's $4^{th}$, $5^{th}$ or $6^{th}$ Amendment rights are admissible for impeachment purposes as long as the statements are not obtained under duress.

**2. Showing Bias**
Bias is showing that a witness has an interest in the outcome in the suit. Having an interest in a suit could be personal, financial or penal. In order to show bias, one must first be asked about the facts that show bias on cross-examination. If the witness admits to the facts, it is within the judge's discretion to admit further extrinsic evidence to prove the bias.

**3. Sensory Defects**
A witness may be impeached by showing that he had no knowledge of the facts for which he is testifying. Impeachment by sensory defect is shown on cross-examination by illustrating the witness's blindness, deafness, intoxication or loss of memory.

**4. Character Evidence**
- **Reputation and Opinion Impeachment Character Evidence**
  A party could, using character traits for untruthfulness, impeach a witness using reputation or opinion evidence.

- **Impeachment By Bad Acts**
  A party could impeach a witness using prior unconvicted bad acts relating to the truthfulness of the witness. However, inquiries into the witness's untruthful bad acts must be based on good faith questioning. If the witness denies any of the untruthful bad acts all questioning must cease (on that issue) and no other witnesses can testify to contradict the witness's denial.

- **Impeachment using Convictions**

  a.  **Felony Convictions**
      Felonies are crimes punishable by death or
      imprisonment in excess of one year. A
      witness can be impeached using past
      convictions if the conviction is less than ten
      years old and the court determines that its
      probative value is outweighed by its
      prejudicial effect for admissibility purposes.

  b.  **Convicted Crimes Bearing on
      Untruthfulness**
      A witness may be impeached using
      conviction of crimes involving dishonesty
      and false statement, irrespective of whether
      the crime is a felony or a misdemeanor.
      However, the conviction must be less than
      ten years old.  Additionally, the judge has
      no discretion to exclude such evidence for
      having a prejudicial effect.

E.  **Rehabilitation of the Witness**
    When the credibility of a witness has been weakened by
    impeachment, it may be rehabilitated. This is done by
    showing a witness's good character or by introducing prior
    consistent statements to rebut a charge of recent fabrication.
    However, a party may not bolster the testimony of his
    witness unless that witness has been impeached.

V.  **INTERROGATION AND PRESENTATION OF
    EVIDENCE**

A.  **Direct and Cross-Examination**
    Each party presents its side of the case. The judge is the
    arbitrator and makes determinations on the evidence
    presented.  Direct examination is the first questioning of a
    witness in a trial or other proceeding conducted by the party
    who called the witness to testify.  Leading questions are not

permitted on direct examination. Leading questions are questions that suggest an answer to the witness being interrogated. However, there are a few exceptions where leading questions could be asked on direct examination. For example, leading questions are permitted on direct examination on preliminary or introductory matters, if the witness is hostile or adverse or if the witness needs assistance in order to respond.

Cross-examination is the formal questioning of a witness by the party opposed to the party who called the witness to testify. On cross-examination, one is permitted to ask leading questions but they are limited to those questions covered on direct or that go to the witness's credibility.

**B. Present Recollection Refreshed**

The law of evidence allows a witness's memory to be enhanced by showing the witness a document that describes the relevant events. The document itself is merely a memory stimulus and is not admitted into evidence. The document that is used to refresh the witness's memory must be related to the subject matter at hand and the adverse party may inspect the writing, cross-examine the witness on the writing, and even introduce it into evidence if it relates to the witness's testimony.

### C. Present Recollection Refreshed Compared to Past Recollection Recorded Ψ

| Refreshed Recollection | Past Recollection Recorded (Hearsay Exception) |
|---|---|
| Witness lacks full recollection of the event. | Witness lacks full recollection of the event. |
| A writing may be used to retrieve the recollection. | A writing may be used to refresh recollection. |
| Any writing may be used to prompt memory. | An accurate writing made by the witness or adopted by witness while it was fresh in his mind may be shown to witness. |
| The writing generally may not be read into evidence. | The writing could be read to the jury but cannot be introduced by the proponent as a substitute for memory. |
| Not considered hearsay | Exception to the hearsay rule. |

## VI.    OPINION TESTIMONY

### A. Lay Person Opinion Testimony
A lay person acting as a witness may state an opinion or give inference when testifying, if such testimony is rationally based on the perception of a witness, helpful to clear an understanding of a witness's testimony or to determine a fact at issue. For example, a lay person could give an opinion as to the following: a person's general appearance, a person's emotional state, the speed of a car, another's intoxication or handwriting. However, a lay person may not give legal conclusions because they require expert opinion.

### B. Experts' Opinion Testimony
Opinions of experts are admissible in the following situations: (1) when the expert opinion assists the trier of fact; (2) when the testimony is based on matters which the expert might reasonably rely; (3) where the expert has

personal knowledge of the subject matter; (4) when the
expert reasonably relied upon facts that experts reasonably
rely on; or (4) the expert is qualified in the subject either by
education or experience. The expert, however, is not
required to disclose her reason for her opinion, but may be
required to do so on cross-examination.

## C. Expert Testimony on Ultimate Issues

Expert testimony is permissible even if it addresses the
ultimate issue in the case. However, in a criminal case, the
expert cannot render an opinion as to the mental state of a
defendant.

## VII. PRIVILEGES

A privilege is a rule of law intended to protect a relationship or
an interest of the person claiming the privilege. Privileges
generally permit one person to refuse to disclose and prohibit
others from disclosing certain types of confidential information
in a judicial proceeding. Although the Federal Rules of
Evidence do not have any specific privilege provisions, three are
recognized by the courts:

### A. The Attorney Client Privilege

The attorney client privilege is the client's right to refuse to
disclose and to prevent any other person from disclosing
confidential communications between himself and his
attorney. Unless the client waives the privilege, it will
continue after the representation stops and continues even
after the client dies (e.g., brought by a successor in interest).
The following are requirements for one to assert the attorney
client privilege:

#### 1. A Confidential Communication

The client must intend the communication to his attorney
to be confidential. If a third party is listening or the
client asks his attorney to disclose the confidential
communication, there is no confidential communication.

2. **Communication Between an Attorney and a Client or his Agent**
The attorney must be a member of the bar or the client must reasonably believe he is a member of the bar. A client is a person seeking consolation from an attorney.

3. **The Communication is Made During Consultation**
The communication is made during an exchange between the client and the attorney where the attorney seeks out the advice of the attorney.

B. **Marital Communication**
The privilege against spousal communications allows a witness spouse to refuse to testify about confidential communications made with his/her spouse during the marriage.

C. **The Difference Between Spousal Immunity and the Marital Privilege** Ψ

| Spousal Immunity | Marital Communication (Privilege) |
|---|---|
| Used only in criminal cases. | Used in both civil and criminal cases. |
| No confidential communication is needed. | Confidential communication needed during marriage. |
| After divorce spouse could testify as to matters learned before and during marriage. | After divorce a spouse cannot testify as to matters learned during marriage. |
| In federal criminal court, witness spouse has privilege. | Either spouse has privilege. |

## VIII. HEARSAY

### A. Hearsay Definition

A hearsay statement is an out of court statement made by one other than the declarant on the stand which is offered into evidence to prove the truth of the matter asserted therein and which is inadmissible in court. An "out of court statement" is a statement made outside the present proceeding or hearing. The "declarant" is the one making the statement. "To prove the truth of the matter asserted" means that the statement is being offered to prove that the contents of the statement are true. The purpose of the hearsay rule is to prevent unreliable or inaccurate information from being introduced in court. Although hearsay statements are inadmissible in court, there are many exceptions to the hearsay rule.

### B. Non-Hearsay Exceptions to the Hearsay Rule

#### 1. Prior Statements of Witnesses

A prior statement of a witness is defined as a prior statement by the witness which is being introduced in court and where the witness is present at trial and subject to cross-examination. There are three types of prior statements of witnesses:

- **Prior Inconsistent Statements**
  This is where the witness on the stand has made prior statements that are inconsistent with his current statements in a judicial proceeding. If the prior statement is sworn, that statement may be introduced to impeach the witness <u>and</u> as substantive evidence. If the prior statement is not sworn the statements may <u>only</u> be used to impeach the witness and <u>not</u> as substantive evidence.

- **Prior Consistent statements**
  Prior consistent statements, whether sworn or unsworn, are inadmissible for the purpose of rebutting a charge of recent fabrication, improper influence or motive.

- **Prior Eyewitness Identification**
  This is where a prior statement of a witness identifying a person (after perceiving him) is introduced when the witness is on the stand. The statement may be sworn or unsworn and may be used to rehabilitate the witness. It may also be used as substantive evidence.

2. **Admissions**
   Admissions are voluntary acknowledgments of the existence of facts relevant to an adversary's case. With respect the hearsay rule, there are four types of admissions:

   - **Party Opponent Admissions**
     A party opponent admission is an admission that a party has previously made manifesting its belief in a statement which includes guilty pleas.

   - **Adoptive Admissions**
     An adoptive admission is an admission where the party opponent was silent, but the circumstances where such that a reasonable person would not have been silent. An admission by silence is admissible if the statement was heard and understood by the listener. Additionally, the subject matter must be within the listener's sphere of knowledge. Lastly, the statement must have been of the type that would have been denied as untrue (if it was, in fact, untrue) when made.

- **Vicarious Admissions**

  A vicarious statement is admissible against a principle if the statement was made by the party's agent, servant, or employee concerning a matter within the scope of the agency or employment and made during the existence of the employment relationship.

- **Co-conspirator Admissions**

  A co-conspirator statement is a statement made by a co-conspirator and admissible against the other co-conspirator if the statement was made during the course of, and in furtherance of, the conspiracy.

3. **Legally Operative Words**

   Legally operative words are words which have legal significance aside from their truth. The issue is whether or not the words were spoken (includes tortuous and transactional words). An example of tortuous words are actual words of slander or liable in defamation cases used to prove defamation. Transactional words are actual words of offer and acceptance used to prove a contract or words of intent used to prove an intent to transfer a will or deed.

C. **Hearsay Exceptions – Availability of the Declarant is Immaterial Ψ**

There are many hearsay exceptions under the Federal Rules of Evidence. The following are the most frequently tested hearsay exceptions where the availability of the declarant is <u>immaterial</u>:

1. **Present Sense Impressions**

   A present sense impression is a statement of an event made as it is occurring or soon after it has occurred.  The statement must describe or explain the event and is made contemporaneously with the perception.

## 2. Excited Utterances

Excited utterances are admissible statements made after a traumatic event. The rational is that the declarant is unlikely to make a false statement after witnessing a startling event. The stress that caused the statement must have caused the declarant to make the statement and the statement must have been made while the declarant was still under the stress (the statement could have been uttered after the startling event, but while the declarant was still under stress of the event).

## 3. Statements about State of Mind

These statements are statements about the declarant's state of mind, emotions, physical condition, future intent or present medical condition(s). Additionally, these statements come into evidence as substantive evidence to prove the existence of the condition.

## 4. Statements of Medical Diagnosis or Treatment

Statements of medical diagnosis or treatment are statements that are about a party's medical condition. The statements must be made concerning past or present symptoms and for the purposes of medical diagnosis or treatment. Statements of present symptoms are admissible even if not made to a physician. Statements of past physical symptoms are only admissible if made to a physician.

## 5. Past Recollection Recorded

A past recollection recorded is when a party makes a record of a recollection at the time of or soon after an event took place and that party could not recall the event when called to testify. The party may then be shown a record to jog his memory of the event. If the record is accurate, it may become part of the evidence presented.

### 6. Business Records

The business records exception states that any writing or record made as a record of an act, transaction, occurrence or event, if within the regular course of business, is admissible as an exception to the hearsay rule.

## D. Hearsay Exceptions – Declarant must be Unavailable Ψ

A declarant is unavailable if he is dead or mentally defective, outside the jurisdiction of the court, refuses to testify, cannot remember or invokes a privilege. The following hearsay exceptions require the declarant to be unavailable:

### 1. Former Testimony

Former testimony is admissible if the party against whom the testimony is now offered was under oath and had the opportunity and similar motive to develop testimony by direct, cross or redirect examination of the declarant.

### 2. Dying Declaration

In order for a dying declaration to be admissible in court, all of the following elements must be met:

- It must be introduced in a civil matter or a homicide criminal case only.
- The declarant must believe that he is about to die or that his death is imminent.
- The statement must concern the cause or the circumstances of what the declarant believes to be his impending death.
- The declarant need not eventually die, but must be competent as a witness if alive to testify.

### 3. Declarations Against Interests

Declarations against interests are statements made by a non-party against his interests that would subject him to

criminal or civil liability. The statement must be that
which a reasonable person in the same position would
not have made unless it was true. Furthermore, the
declarant must have personal knowledge of the facts
asserted, be aware the statement was against his interest
and have no motive for misrepresentation. Additionally,
the statement must be corroborated to be admissible.

## E. Hearsay within Hearsay

When one out of court statement is offered for its truth and
contains another out of court statement, each piece of
hearsay must have its own exception to be admissible. For
example, if a police report (assumed to be hearsay) contains
a statement by a witness that is hearsay, both the police
report and the hearsay statement must have an exception to
be admissible.

## F. Residual Exception

The residual exception to the hearsay rule is a catchall
exception permitting the admission of evidence that is
trustworthy but does not fall within any of the other
recognized exceptions. The court takes into account the
following when determining whether a statement is
admissible under this rule: (1) whether the statement was
made under oath; (2) if the time lapse between the event and
the statement was short; and (3) the motivation of the
declarant to speak truthfully.

# CONTRACTS

## I. INTRODUCTION

### A. The Agreement Process

In order for a valid contract to be formed, the parties must form an agreement by consenting to the same terms at the same time. The purpose of the contract is to give effect to the reasonable expectations of the parties to the agreement. This is accomplished by the process of offer, acceptance and consideration.

### B. Contracts in General

#### 1. Express Contracts

If the offer and acceptance are manifested by oral or written words, the resulting bargain is an express contract.

#### 2. Implied Contracts

Here the mutual assent of the parties is manifested by conduct rather than oral or written words.

#### 3. Quasi-contracts

A quasi-contract is a contract created by common law to avoid unjust enrichment of a person who has received the benefit of the bargain.

#### 4. Unilateral and Bilateral Contracts

A unilateral contract is a contract in which one party makes a promise or undertakes a performance. A bilateral contract is a contract in which each party promises performance so that each party is an obligator on his own promise and the obligee on the other's promise.

**5. Executed and Executory Contracts**

Executory contracts are contracts that remain wholly unperformed or for which there remains something still to be done on both sides. An executed contract is a contract that is fully performed by both sides.

**6. Void and Voidable Contracts Ψ**

A contract that is void is a contract that has no legal effect from the onset. By contrast, a voidable contract is where one or both parties to the contract could elect to avoid the contract because of physical defects.

**7. UCC Contracts**

Article 2 of the Uniform Commercial Code (UCC) applies to all contracts for the sale of goods, including distributorships or franchises.

## II.  THE OFFER

### A. The Elements of an Offer: Ψ

**1. Intent to be legally bound**

The offeror must intend to be legally bound upon acceptance. The offeror's intent is measured by an objective standard which requires an examination of the relationship of the parties, the words of commitment between the parties, and the surrounding circumstances to determine if a reasonable person would have intended to be bound. The following are invitations and not intentions to be bound:

- Offers made in jest
- Preliminary negotiations
- Statements of intention
- Mere inquiries
- Auctions or bid solicitations
- Advertisements
- Rewards to the public

## 2. The Contract Terms are Definite

The more definite and certain the terms of a contract are, the more reasonable it is that an offer took place. If some terms are left open, the contract will not fail for indefiniteness if the parties intended to make a contract. Similarly, where a UCC contract leaves some terms open, the contract will not fail for indefiniteness if the parties intended to make a contract.

- The essential terms of a contract under the common law are:
  1. The offer must clearly identify the parties to the contract.
  2. The price must be agreed upon (but if a price is not mentioned, a reasonable price will be assumed at the time of delivery).
  3. The time of performance must be stated.
  4. The subject matter of the contract must include the quantity and the nature of the work performed.

- The essential terms for UCC contracts:
  1. The parties to the contract; and
  2. The quantity of the subject matter.

  Under the UCC, the price and the time for performance could be reasonably implied.

## 3. Communication of Intent

The offer must be communicated to the offeree or his agent and the offeree must know of the offer before he can act on it.

## B. Termination of an Offer

### 1. Termination by Offeror

The offeror may revoke an offer at any time before acceptance. Termination occurs via death, lapse of reasonable time before acceptance or by communication. Revocation by the offeror by communication could be done directly or indirectly. Direct revocation by communication is where the revocation is communicated orally or in writing to the offeree with the intent of revocation. Indirect revocation by the offeror is done by communicating information that is inconsistent with the offer; such as telling a third party that he no longer has the subject matter of the offer and the third party tells the offeree.

There are four irrevocable offers that once made cannot be revoked. They are:

1. **Option Contracts**

   Option contracts are agreements to hold an offer open for a fixed period of time.
   Acceptance must be received prior to the option expiration. If there is delay in acceptance due to the offeror, then a reasonable time beyond the option period is granted.

2. **Firm Offers**

   Under the UCC, firm offers are signed written offers made by a merchant to another merchant or non-merchant which is irrevocable for the time stated, or if no time is stated, for a reasonable time not to exceed three months.

   Both option contracts and firm offers stay open until the expiration of the time stated, the destruction of the subject matter, a subsequent illegality or by an outright rejection by the offeree if relied upon by the offeror who acts to his detriment.

   Additionally, the following do not terminate option contracts or firm offers:

   1. Counter offers
   2. Attempted revocation by the offeror
   3. Death or insanity

4. Unrelied upon rejection by the offeree

### 3. Offers Detrimentally Relied Upon

Detrimental reliance, the third irrevocable offer, is reliance by one party on the acts or representations of another, causing a worsening of the first party's position.

### 4. Promissory Estoppel

Promissory estoppel is the principle that a promise made without consideration becomes binding if: (1) the promisor intends or should reasonable expect the promise to induce reliance; (2) a party actually relies on the promise; and (3) non-enforcement of the promise will cause detriments injury or injustice.

## 2. Termination by Offeree

Termination of an offer by the offeree can be done either by rejection or counter offer and is effective when received. Rejection could either be express and directly or indirectly communicated by offeree or by conduct that would be consistent with a rejection. An offeree could also reject an offer by a counter offer. A counter offer is an offer made by the offeree to the offeror in response to the offer which is not an acceptance, but a change in the terms of the offer.

## 3. Termination of an Offer by Operation of Law

In addition to an offer being terminated by the offeror or offeree, an offer could also be terminated by operation of law. The following are ways an offer is terminated by operation of law:

- Lapse of reasonable time between offer and acceptance.
- Death or disability before acceptance.
- Destruction of subject matter.
- Subsequent illegality.

## III.   ACCEPTANCE
The following are the elements of acceptance:

**1   Acceptance may only be made by the party to whom the offer is addresses or his agent. Ψ**
An offer to contract is unique to the person to whom it is addressed and may not be assigned. However, option contracts may be assigned because they are binding contracts.

**2   Acceptance must meet the conditions of the offer and be unconditional.**
The offeror is in control of the terms of the contract and the offeree must accept the contract only on those terms. This is called the **Mirror Image Rule**. In addition, if there is an attempt to change the terms of the offer, e.g. the offeree has made a counter offer, it becomes a rejection of the original offer.

The UCC however does not follow the mirror image rule. Under the UCC any acceptance that shows intent to contract is an acceptance. When there are additions to the contract and either the offeror or offeree is a non-merchant, the terms of the offer govern for acceptance. Additional or different terms to the offer do not become part of the contract unless agreed to by the offeror. If both the offeree and the offeror are merchants, additional or different terms do become part of the contract unless objected to within a reasonable time or they materially alter the offer. This is called the **Battle of the Forms**.

When the method of acceptance is unclear and the offeree controls the method of acceptance, a doubtful offer is made. In such a case, the offeree controls the method of acceptance.

3   **The offeree must know of the offer before acceptance.**
    The offeree must know of the offer before he can accept it.
    If the offeree completes performance and then finds out
    about the offer, there is no acceptance.

4   **Acceptance must be communicated to the offeror. Ψ**
    Acceptance will depend on whether the offer is unilateral or
    bilateral. Unilateral contracts require full performance and
    bilateral contracts require communication for acceptance.

    Generally, an acceptance received by the offeror is valid and
    concludes a contract. However, under the **Mailbox Rule**,
    acceptance is effective upon dispatch, not receipt. The
    mailbox rule states that if the offeree used the same or
    similar means of communication as the offeror, the
    acceptance is effective on dispatch. A rejection of the offer is
    effective only upon receipt. There are situations where the
    mailbox rule is not applicable. For example, if the offer
    states the desired method of communication, the mailbox
    rule does not apply. Additionally, acceptance of an option
    contract or a firm offer must be received within the stated
    period of time to be effective. If the acceptance is
    dispatched outside the time frame of acceptance, the
    Mailbox rule does not apply. Most importantly, the mailbox
    rule is not applicable if the offeree sends an acceptance and
    then sends a rejection to overtake the acceptance. This is
    called the **vacillating offeree problem** and it constitutes an
    acceptance unless the rejection is received first and the
    offeror has detrimentally relied on the rejection.

IV.   **CONSIDERATION**
      Generally, consideration is the bargained for legal exchange of
      something of value. Consideration requires three elements: (1)
      the promisee must suffer a legal detriment because of the
      promise; (2) the promisee's detriment must induce the promise;
      and (3) the promise must induce the promisee's detriment. Some
      promises are not supported by a bargained for exchange of value
      and therefore unenforceable. A promise supported by past

consideration is unenforceable because the detriment did not induce the promise since the detriment had already occurred and was not bargained for in exchange for the promise. Additionally, the **preexisting duty rule** states there is no consideration where there is a promise to do an act that that one is already obligated to do. If one already has a legal obligation to do some act, he cannot use that act as consideration for another promise.

However, there are some exceptions to the pre-existing duty rule. First, if new or different consideration is given for an act one is already obligated to do, the promise does not fail for lack of a bargained for exchange. Second, if unforeseen difficulties arise and neither party had assumed the risk, the contract could be rescinded. Only then could new and different consideration be used as compensation for the unforeseen difficulty. Third, if there is an honest, good faith dispute over the terms of the promise, then the new consideration to do the same act is adequate consideration for resolving the dispute. Under the UCC, however, the preexisting duty rule does not apply. Instead the UCC states that all contract modifications are enforceable if they are done in good faith and do not violate the Statute of Frauds.

Contract law also recognizes consideration "substitutes." First, at common law if a promise was in writing, sealed and delivered, consideration was not needed. Second, some jurisdictions hold that a writing is presumed to be supported by consideration. This means that if a party produces a writing stating an agreement was entered into, it is presumed that the writing was supported by consideration. The third consideration substitute is detrimental reliance, which is when there is reliance by one party on the acts or representations of another, causing a worsening of the first party's position. If one party detrimentally relies on a promise, that reliance is a substitute for consideration because an injustice would arise if the promise were not enforceable due to a lack of consideration. Promissory estoppel is the last consideration substitute. Promissory estoppel, as stated earlier, is the principle that a promise made without consideration becomes

binding if: (1) the promisor intends or should reasonable expect
the promise to induce reliance, (2) the party actually relies on the
promise, and (3) the non-enforcement of the promise will cause a
party injury or injustice. Thus, if a promisee has reasonably
relied on a promise to his detriment, the promisor is estopped
from denying that the promise lacked consideration.

## V.     TYPES OF CONTRACTS  Ψ

### 1. Joint and Several Contracts
Joint and several contracts are contracts between two or more
parties which promise the same promise to the promisee and
where each is bound for the whole performance.

### 2. Divisible Contracts
Divisible contracts are contracts that can be apportioned into
corresponding parts of performance.  If there is a breach in
one part, it can be severed and the balance of the contract is
enforceable.

### 3. Output Contracts
Output contracts are contracts in which the buyer promises to
buy all the goods or services that a seller can supply during a
specified period at a set price.

### 4. Requirement Contracts
Requirement contracts are contracts in which a seller
promises to supply all the goods or services that a buyer
needs during a specific period and at a set price, and where
the buyer promises to obtain those goods or services
exclusively from the seller.

## VI.    DEFENSES TO FORMATION AND ENFORCEMENT OF
CONTRACTS

### A.  Lack of Capacity

#### 1.  Minors
Minors may form contracts. However, their obligations
are voidable (could be disaffirmed). Most jurisdictions

hold the age of majority at 18 in contrast to the common law age of 21.

A contract made during one's age of minority could be disaffirmed at any time before or after reaching one's majority. The way one disaffirms a contract is to objectively signify the intention to avoid the contract. Once a contract is disaffirmed, the minor is obligated to the other party for restitution. If services were conferred to the minor, the minor has no obligation to make restitution. However, if goods are conferred, the minor must return them.

A contract made during one's minority could also be affirmed once reaching the age of majority by making a new promise to assume the liabilities of the contract. The way one affirms a contract is by demonstrating an objective intention to assume the contract.

**2. Disability**
Contracts made by persons suffering from a mental disability are voidable.

**3. Corporate contracts**
Contracts entered into by corporations which are *ultra vires* are voidable. Ultra vires corporate acts are acts that are beyond the power of the corporation. Corporations are analogous to persons, contractually speaking. Sometimes corporations, like people, are unable to enter into contracts.

**B. Illegality**
Contracts could be illegal if the subject matter violates a statute or if so declared by a court and thus serve as a defense to formation. If the subject matter is illegal at the time of the formation of the agreement, there is no offer and the contract is void. If the offer is made and the subject matter subsequently becomes illegal before acceptance, the offer is

terminated by operation of law. If the subject matter becomes illegal after there is acceptance, the obligations of both are discharged without a legal remedy due to the impossibility of performance. In cases where a contract could be divided, some courts allow the severing of the portion of the contract that is illegal and enforcing the remainder of the contract that is legal.

## C. Ambiguity
The ambiguity of a contract serves as a defense. A contract is ambiguous if, at its formation, the parties used words or phrases that have more than one reasonable meaning and each party attached a different meaning to it. If the different meanings go to the essential terms of the contract, there is a defense to the formation of the contract.

## D. Mistake
There are two types of mistakes, mutual mistakes and unilateral mistakes. Mutual mistakes are mistakes made by both parties, whereas unilateral mistakes are mistakes made by one party. In the case of mutual mistakes, if the mistake negates the basic intentions of the parties and the mistake goes to a material part of the contract, the contract could be avoided by either party. However in the case of unilateral mistakes, the mistake will only be a defense if a party knew or should have known of the mistake. If there is a unilateral mistake and one of the parties is unaware of the mistake and goes through with the contract, a valid contract is formed unless the contract is unconscionable.

## E. Duress
Duress is the coercive force used to compel another to contract against his will or judgment. There are two types of duress: physical and economic duress. Physical duress is when physical coercive acts or threats of acts are used to induce another's consent to a contract. In contrast, economic duress is the unlawful coercion to contract by threatening financial injury at a time when one cannot exercise free will.

## F.  Undue Influence
Undue influence is the unfair or improper persuasion of one person by another who has attained the position of fiduciary.

## G.  Fraud
Fraud is the knowing misrepresentation of the truth or concealment of a material fact to induce another to act to his injury.  There are three types of fraud: (1) fraud in the factum occurs when a legal instrument as actually executed differs from the one intended for execution by the person who executed it.  For example, when a blind person signs a mortgage and is falsely told that it is just a letter, there is fraud in the factum.  (2) fraud in the inducement is when misrepresentations lead another to enter into a contract with a false impression of the risks or obligations involved.  (3) fraud in the execution exists when the victim is aware the contract is formed but after the contract is reduced to writing and signed, the contract is found to be the product of the selective or inventive memory of the drafter.

## H.  The Doctrine of Unconscionability
The doctrine of unconscionability holds that a court may refuse to enforce a contract that is unfair or oppressive because of procedural abuses during contract formation or due to the overreaching contractual terms.  Overreaching contractual terms are terms that are unreasonably favorable to one party while precluding a meaningful choice for the other party.

## I.  Statute of Frauds

### Introduction
The statute of frauds is a statute based on English law that prevents fraud by requiring certain contracts to be in writing and signed by the parties.  The statute of frauds applies to the following:

1. **Contracts made in consideration of marriage**
   An agreement made upon consideration of marriage, other than the mutual promise to marry, must be in writing and signed by the promisor to be enforceable.

2. **Contracts not to be performed within one year**
   An agreement by its terms not to be performed within one year from the <u>date of formation</u> must be in writing and signed. However, if there is a possibility that that the contract could be performed within one year, the statute of frauds does not apply.

3. **Contracts Transferring Land**
   Any agreement for the transfer of land or any fixture permanently attached to the land, must be in writing and signed by the party charged. This includes agreements for the lease of real property for <u>more</u> than one year. Leases for one year or less are normally not with in the statute of frauds. The time is measured from the time the lease commences <u>not</u> from the time the agreement is made.

4. **Contracts of an Executor or Administrator to Answer for a Decedent's Debt**
   Agreements that make executors or administrators liable for a decedent's debts must be in writing and signed to be enforceable.

5. **Contracts for the Sale of Goods Valued at $500 or More**
   Under the UCC, contracts for the sale of goods that are valued at $500 or more must be in writing and signed by the party charged. There are, however, a few exceptions. First, if the seller has tendered goods and the buyer has accepted them, the agreed upon price is enforceable despite the contract being oral. Second, if the oral contract is for specially manufactured goods not suitable for resale, the oral contract is enforceable. Finally, under

the **Merchant Memo Rule**, if a contact is between merchants, a written confirmation of its terms sent by one party and received by the other is enforceable unless objected to within ten days.

### 6. Surety or Guarantee Contracts

Any promises to answer for the debts of another must be in writing and signed by the parties charged. However, if the purpose of the contract is for the benefit of the promisor, it is not considered a debt of another person and is not subject to the statute of frauds.

## EXCEPTIONS TO THE STATUTE OF FRAUDS

### 1. Equitable Estoppel

If the other party relied to their detriment on a promise, the oral agreement is enforceable and the statute of frauds cannot be used as a defense.

### 2. Full or Part Performance

Contracts that have been fully performed by both sides (parties) are not subject to the statute of frauds. With respect to a contract for the sale of goods, only that part performed is exempt from the statute of frauds and is enforceable. In the case of the sale of land, if the buyer has taken possession of the land and either made valuable or permanent improvements or paid the full purchase price, the contract is not subject to the statute of frauds.

### 3. Admissions in Pleadings or Court

If the party against whom enforcement of a contract is sought admits in pleadings or in testimony that the contract was made, the contract is enforceable.

### 4. Third Parties

The statute of frauds defense is only available to the parties of the contract, not to third parties.

### 5. UCC Exceptions
As mentioned earlier, the UCC exceptions to the statute of frauds are the merchant memo rule and specially manufactured goods.

## VII. PAROLE EVIDENCE
The parole evidence rule holds that if the parties to a contract have reduced their agreement to a writing, intended as the full and final expression of their agreement, then any evidence (whether written or oral) of prior contemporaneous promises or understandings is irrelevant to modify, add to or contradict the terms of that writing.

Only writings that are intended as a final expression of the parties are protected by the parole evidence rule. If the writing is the final expression of the parties, the writing is said to be integrated. The burden is on the party seeking to invoke the rule to prove that the writing was mutual. The easiest way to determine if the writing is the final expression of the parties is to see if there is an **integration or merger clause** at the end of the contract. An integration clause is a clause that states that the writing is the final expression of the parties.

Parole evidence is only precluded if it modifies, adds to or contradicts the terms of the agreement. However, parole evidence may be used to clarify a mistake or ambiguity, explain the agreement, establish collateral agreements or to prove trade custom or course of dealings.

## VIII. CONTRACT MODIFICATION
A contract modification can raise two issues: (1) lack of consideration for the modification; and (2) the statute of frauds.

### 1. Lack of Consideration for the Modification
Under common law, the preexisting duty rule required new or different consideration for a contract modification. However,

under the UCC, no consideration is needed for a written or oral modification made in good faith.

## 2. Statute of Frauds

The statute of frauds could raise an issue with respect to contract modifications. Under contract law, the contract as modified must satisfy the statute of frauds (a writing is needed for the modification).

## IX. THIRD PARTY BENEFICIARIES

A third party beneficiary is a person who is not a party to a contract, but who may benefit from the contract's performance.

## 1. Incidental Third Party Beneficiary

An incidental beneficiary is a third party beneficiary who is not intended to benefit from the contract and thus does not acquire rights under the contract.

## 2. Intended Third Party Beneficiary

An intended beneficiary is a third party who is intended to benefit from a contract and thus acquires rights under the contract, including the ability to enforce the contract once those rights have vested. A third party is intended if (1) he is named in the contract or reasonably relies on the promise; (2) performance runs directly to the third party; or (3) the promisee intends that the benefit run to the third party. Once the party is determined to be "intended" it must be decided whether the party is a creditor or donee beneficiary.

- **Creditor Beneficiary**
  A creditor beneficiary is a party that the promisee intends to discharge some obligation upon. If the party is determined to be a creditor beneficiary, it could sue both the promisor and the promisee on the contract.

- **Donee Beneficiary**
  A donee beneficiary is a party that the promisee intends to confer a gift upon. If the party is

determined to be a donee beneficiary, it could <u>only</u> sue the promisee on the contract.

### 3. Vesting

The intended beneficiary could only institute a suit on the contract if his rights vest. An intended beneficiary's rights vest when the third party learns and assents to the contract. Assent could be inferred if the third party institutes a suit or if there is detrimental reliance.

## X. ASSIGNMENT AND DELEGATION

Assignments and delegations are attempts by one party to an existing contract to substitute a third party for its position in the contract.

### 1. Assignment

An assignment requires the assignor, the person who transfers the contract right to another, to clearly intend to transfer completely his rights under an existing contract to a third party. The effect of an assignment is to create privity of contract between the assignee (the person to whom the assignment is made) and the obligator (the person obligated under the contract).

Generally, all rights are assignable <u>except</u> for future rights. There are, however, a few exceptions to this rule. Rights may not be assigned if the agreement prohibits the assignment, if the assignment will cause a substantial change in the performance or if there is a statutory provision prohibiting the assignment.

Under the UCC, a contract prohibiting an assignment is void with two exceptions. First, an assignment for requirement or an output contract is valid if a business is being sold to a new owner with such a contract. Second, if the contract requires a personal element, it cannot be assigned if there is a provision restricting assignment.

Assignments can be made orally with the following exceptions. First, assignments affecting an interest in land are not orally assignable as against the statute of frauds. Second, assignments for the sale of goods valued at $500 or more violate the statute of frauds. Third, wage assignments are not orally assignable. Finally, assignments intended as a security interest are not orally assignable.

Both oral and written assignments for consideration are irrevocable. However, gratuitous assignments are revocable with the following exceptions: (1) the assignment is in writing; or (2) the assignee has detrimentally relied on the assignment; or (3) the performance of the obligator has already been performed; or (4) the assignee has delivered a writing representing the assignment.

After the assignment, the assignee of the contract holds all the rights of the assignor. Additionally, the obligator can raise any defense against the assignor as long as the defense arose prior to the notice of the assignment to the obligator.

Although both assignments and third party beneficiaries accomplish the same goal, they are different. In a contract involving a third party beneficiary, the parties to the contract intend the benefits to run to the third party. In an assignment, the assignee is introduced subsequent to the contract after the assignor transfers his rights to him (assignee).

## 2. Delegation

A delegation of a contract duty is the entrusting of another with authority or empowering another to act as his agent or representative. Delegation agreements require the obligee to agree to assume the duty and the obligee becomes a third party beneficiary of the promise of the delegatee.

All duties may be delegated with the exception of contracts that prohibit delegation, laws that prohibit delegation, if the delegation changes the obligee's expectancy or if the delegation requires personal judgment or skill.

## XI.   WARRANTIES

In order to increase consumer protection, the UCC has incorporated certain express and implied warranties as part of a contract.

### 1. Express Warranties

Express warranties can be made by merchants or non-merchants by an affirmative fact or promise, using a sample or model of the goods or by a description of the goods as part of the bargain. "Puffery," however, does not constitute an express warranty. Puffery is the bolstering of the value of the goods based on opinion.

### 2. Warranty Against Infringement

A warranty against infringement is when a merchant who deals in goods of a certain kind warrants that the goods are free from encumbrances.

### 3. Implied Warranty of Merchantability

An implied warranty of merchantability is when a merchant who sells goods warrants that goods are merchantable.

### 4. Implied Warranty of Fitness for a Particular Purpose

An implied warranty for a particular purpose is when:

(1) a merchant or a non-merchant sells particular goods;
(2) has actual or constructive knowledge of the purpose for which the buyer is buying the particular goods; and
(3) the buyer relies on the seller's skill in buying the goods.

## Comparison Chart Ψ

| Warranty | What it Warrants | Merchant or Non-merchant | Disclaimers |
|---|---|---|---|
| Express Warranty | Affirmative fact or promise as to goods | Applies to merchants or non-merchants | General disclaimers are unenforceable |
| Implied Warranty Against Infringement | Goods are being delivered free from encumbrances | Applies only to merchants | General disclaimers are unenforceable |
| Implied Warranty of Merchantability | Goods are merchantable | Applies only to merchants | General Disclaimers are enforceable |
| Implied Warranty of Fitness for a Particular Purpose | Seller has knowledge of buyer's purpose of the goods and buyer relies on seller's skill | Applies to merchants or non-merchants | General disclaimers are enforceable |

There are, however, limitations on warranty protections. Some states allow warranty protections to extend to any natural person who is in the family or in the household of the buyer or a guest in the buyer's home. Other states allow any natural person who may reasonably be expected to use the goods to be protected by the warranty of the goods.

There are many defenses to a breach of warranty claim. If a party assumes the risk of the use of the goods, then the seller may have a defense. There is also a statute of limitations defense if the suit is instituted beyond the proscribed limitations period.

## XII.    EXCUSABLE NON-PERFORMANCE

### 1. Impossibility of Performance Ψ

Impossibility of performance is when the promised performance cannot be done. In order to use a defense of impossibility, it must be demonstrated that before the formation of the contract, the impossible factors were not foreseeable.

### 2. Impracticability of Performance Ψ

Impracticability of performance is when a gross increase in the cost of performance, due to unforeseen developments, makes a contract impracticable to perform, but not when an agreement is impossible to perform.

### 3. Frustration of Purpose Ψ

Frustration of purpose is the doctrine that states that when the performance of a contract becomes fundamentally changed without fault of either party, the contract is considered dissolved. The event that changes the contract must be unforeseen by both parties and must destroy the purpose of the agreement, which both parties knew was the purpose.

## XIII.    MATERIAL AND MINOR BREACHES OF CONTRACTS

Any breach warrants a suit for damages. A material breach discharges the duty of counter performance and the non-breaching party could sue on the entire contract. Minor breaches do not discharge the duty of performance but there still exists a remedy.

### 1. The Perfect Tender Rule Ψ

Where a party substantially performs on a contract, but not the whole contract, there exists a minor breach. A contract is substantially performed when its essential purpose has been met. Under the UCC's perfect tender rule, a buyer, upon inspection, may reject a seller's goods if the quality, quantity or delivery of the goods fails to conform precisely to the contract. If the inspection reveals non-conforming goods, the buyer could reject the whole, accept the whole or accept any commercial unit or units and reject the balance. If the buyer intends to reject the goods, he must seasonably notify the seller of the rejection. If there is no notice of rejection, then there is a *de facto* acceptance of the goods. Also, the seller is given the opportunity to cure the non-conforming tender if the time for the seller's performance has not yet expired.

## 2. Anticipatory Repudiation
An anticipatory repudiation is where a party makes it clear that before performance is due, he does not intend to perform his duties. Anticipatory repudiation can be retracted before the affected party has materially relied on the repudiation or advised the repudiating party that the repudiation is final. Once there is evidence of anticipatory repudiation, the non-breaching party may treat the contract as discharged, sue immediately or suspend performance. Damages on the claim are as of the day of the repudiation, not the day of the actual suit.

Anticipatory repudiation differs from a prospective inability to perform in that a prospective inability to perform arises when a person's conduct, rather than his expression, makes it clear that he will not perform his end of the agreement. In a perspective inability to perform situation, the non-breaching party may demand adequate written assurance of performance. In addition, the non-breaching party may suspend performance of the contract until assurance is given or treat the contract as breached if the insecurity is not resolved within 30 days of the demand.

## XIV. REMEDIES FOR BREACH OF CONTRACT

### A. Interests Protected by Breach of Contract
Since the goal of contract law is to compensate the injured party, punitive damages are not recoverable. When a party suffers a material breach there are at least three interests that are immediately threatened:

1. **Restitution Interest**

   Restitution interests are protected when there is no contract, but where a contract is implied in law or where a contract existed and was rightfully rescinded by the non-breaching party. The goal is to prevent the defendant's unjust enrichment. Restitution is calculated by awarding the defendant the value of his performance if there was no contract.

2. **Expectancy Interest**

   Expectancy interests are used when a contract exists and is used to put the plaintiff in the same position he would have been in had the contract been fulfilled. Expectancy interests are determined by calculating the difference between what was contracted for and what was actually received.

3. **The Reliance Interest**

   Reliance interests are used when a contract exists and expectancy is too hard to prove. It is usually based on promissory estoppel. The goal of the reliance interests is to put the plaintiff in the same position he would have been in if the contract was never entered into. This is calculated by determining the cost to the plaintiff of conferring the value.

B. **The Lost Volume Seller**

   Contract law recognizes a loss of bargain measure of damages. Also called the loss volume seller, this is a seller of goods who, after a buyer has breached a sales contract, resells the goods to a different buyer who would have bought identical goods from the seller's inventory even if the original buyer had not breached. Such a seller is entitled to lost profits rather than the contract price less market price as damages from the original buyer's breach.

### C.  Compensatory Damages
Compensatory damages are damages awarded for the loss of what a person reasonably anticipated to get from the contract but which was not completed.

### D.  Consequential Damages
Consequential damages are losses that do not flow directly and immediately from the injurious act, but rather result indirectly from the act.

### E.  Incidental Damage
Incidental damages are losses reasonably associated with or related to actual damages.

### F.  Liquidated Damages
Liquidated damages are damages which were contractually stipulated to as a reasonable estimation of actual damages to be recovered by one party if the other party breached.

### G.  Specific Performance
Equitable remedies, such as specific performance, are usually only available when legal remedies (money damages) are unavailable. Specific performance is a court ordered remedy that requires precise fulfillment of the contractual obligation.  The requirements of specific performance are:

1.  **That the contract is definite and certain**
    The court will only grant specific performance when it could determine that the terms are certain.

2.  **There is an inadequacy of a remedy at law**
    Specific performance will only be granted if the remedy at law is inadequate. If the remedy at law is adequate, specific performance will not be granted.

3.  **Enforcement must operate equitably**
    Specific performance will be denied if its enforcement will cause great hardship.

### 4. The enforcement must be feasible
If granting specific performance would be unreasonably difficult, the court will not order it.

## H. Damages for UCC Contracts

### 1. Remedies Available to Buyer and Seller
    a. Liquidated damages
    b. Incidental and consequential damages
    c. Anticipatory repudiation
    d. Demand for adequate assurance

### 1. Seller's Remedies
    a. Refuse delivery
    b. Stop goods in transit
    c. Reclaim goods delivered

### 3. Buyer's Remedies
    a. Return of any deposit
    b. Damages
    c. Reject goods
    d. Specific performance
    e. Cover (substituted goods)
    f. Replevin and recoupment

# CRIMINAL LAW

## I. CRIMES GENERALLY

### A. Crime Classifications

**1. Misdemeanor**
A misdemeanor is a crime punishable by imprisonment for less then one year or by a fine.

**2. Felony**
A felony is a crime punishable by death or imprisonment exceeding one year. The following at common law were considered felonies: robbery, burglary, larceny, murder, manslaughter, mayhem and arson.

**3. Malum in Se Crimes**
A malum in se crime is a crime that is wrong in and of itself due to criminal intent or the involvement of moral turpitude. Examples of malum in se crimes are: rape, murder and robbery.

**4. Malum Prohibitum Crimes**
Malum prohibitum crimes are crimes that are prohibited by legislation. Examples of malum prohibitum crimes are: firearm laws, speeding and other traffic infractions.

**5. Infamous Crimes**
At common law, infamous crimes were crimes that involved fraud and dishonesty.

**6. General Intent Crimes Ψ**
General intent crimes require the commission of an unlawful act without specific intent. If the defendant is reckless, negligent, or aware of the risk, he has the general intent to commit the crime. General intent crimes include: depraved heart murder, involuntary

manslaughter, kidnapping, rape, battery, arson and false imprisonment.

### 7. Specific Intent Crimes Ψ

Specific intent crimes involve more than an objective intent in doing the proscribed act; they require a desire to achieve the result. Specific intent crimes include: attempt, solicitation, conspiracy, burglary, robbery, assault, larceny, larceny by trick, intentional murder and voluntary manslaughter.

### 8. Malicious Crimes

Malicious crimes are those crimes where the defendant acts with a reckless disregard for others.

### 9. Strict Liability Crimes Ψ

A strict liability crime is a crime that does not require a mens rea element.

## B. Burdens of Proof

The prosecution has the burden of proving each element of the crime **beyond a reasonable doubt**. The defendant has the burden of proving affirmative defenses by a **preponderance of the evidence**.

## II. ELEMENTS OF A CRIME

In order for a defendant to be guilty of a crime, the prosecution must prove **beyond a reasonable doubt**: (1) Actus rea; (2) Mens rea; (3) Concurrence of actus rea and mens rea; (4) Causation; and (5) Injury.

## A. Actus Reus

The defendant must voluntarily act (actus reus) to be culpable for a crime. Any acts which are reflexive, convulsive, performed while unconscious or are merely bad thoughts are insufficient as they are considered involuntarily acts. Criminal liability could also be imposed on a defendant that <u>fails to act</u> where there is a <u>legal duty to act</u> due to a contract, statute or based on a fiduciary relationship.

## B. Mens Rea Ψ

Mens rea is the state of mind or mental state that the prosecution must prove the defendant had when he committed the crime. The following are the four different mental states:

### 1. Intentional
A defendant intentionally acts when he wants his acts to cause certain consequences or knows that his acts are substantially certain to cause the consequences.

### 2. Knowingly
A defendant acts knowingly when he knows that his conduct will cause a certain result.

### 3. Negligently
A defendant acts negligently if he is aware of a substantial and unjustifiable risk that his conduct is of that nature.

### 4. Recklessly
A defendant acts recklessly if he consciously disregards a substantial and unjustifiable risk that his conduct is of that nature.

## C. Concurrence of Actus Reas and Mens Rea
In order for the defendant to be guilty of a crime, the defendant's criminal intent must occur at the same time he commits the criminal act.

## D. Causation
The defendant's conduct must be both the actual and proximate cause of the crime.

CRIMINAL LAW      LEGAL PATH
MULTISTATE BAR EXAMINATION
REVIEW      CRIMINAL LAW

## E. Injury

The victim must suffer a harm due to the defendant's criminal conduct.

## III. DEFENSES:

### A. Insanity

Each jurisdiction has its own test for insanity. The majority of jurisdictions use the M'Naughton Test while a minority of jurisdictions use the Irresistible Impulse Test, the Substantial Capacity Test or some similar variation.

#### 1. M'Naughton Test

A defendant is relived of criminal liability upon proof that at the time of the act, the defendant had a defect in reason by virtue of a disease of the mind so as not to know the nature or the quality of the act performed or if he did not know what he was doing was wrong.

#### 2. Irresistible Impulse Test

A defendant will be found not guilt by reason of mental disease if he lacked capacity for self-control.

#### 3. Substantial Capacity Test

A defendant is not responsible for his conduct, if at the time of the criminal conduct, the defendant lacked substantial capacity to appreciate the criminality of his conduct or failed to conform his conduct to the law.

### B. Intoxication Ψ

#### 1. Voluntary Intoxication

Voluntary intoxication is only a defense to specific intent crimes if it negates the defendant's intent.

#### 2. Involuntary Intoxication

Involuntary intoxication is a defense to all crimes including strict liability crimes.

### C. Infancy

At common law, infancy was considered a complete defense for children under seven years of age. Children between the ages of seven and fourteen were presumed to lack criminal capacity. Children over the age of fourteen were tried as adults. Today, many states do not follow the common law rules for infancy, but rather establish specific ages for criminal convictions.

### D. Self-Defense

If one has a reasonable belief that he is in imminent danger of bodily harm, he may use that amount of force reasonably necessary to prevent such harm. Deadly force may only be used if one is threatened with death or serious bodily harm; otherwise, only non-deadly force may be used. If one is the aggressor, he does not have the right to self-defense. However, if the aggressor completely withdraws or the victim escalates the force used, he may use the defense of self-defense.

### E. Defense of Others Ψ

A defendant is justified in using force to defend another person if he reasonably believes the victim had the right to use such force.

### F. Defense of Property

One may use reasonable <u>non-deadly</u> force to protect property from theft, destruction or trespass. However, deadly force may <u>never</u> be used to protect property.

### G. Necessity

A defendant is justified to engage in criminal conduct to prevent immediate danger resulting from non-human forces which are necessary to avoid greater harm.

## H. Duress
One may be justified in engaging in criminal conduct if one reasonably believes that it is the only means to avoid unlawful threats of great bodily injury or imminent death.

## I. Entrapment
Entrapment is a defense if the crime is a product of law enforcement and the defendant is <u>not</u> predisposed to committing the crime.

## J. Mistake

### 1. Mistake of Fact Ψ

| Mental state of crime | Application of the defense |
| --- | --- |
| Specific Intent Crimes | Any mistake of fact reasonable or unreasonable is a defense. |
| Malice or General Intent Crimes | Only reasonable mistake of facts are defenses. |
| Strict Liability Crimes | Mistake of facts are never a defense. |

### 2. Mistake of Law
Mistake of law is never a defense unless the criminal statute, which the defendant violated, was not reasonably available to the defendant.

## K. Consent
Consent is never a defense to a crime except when the consent negates a specific element of the offense (such as rape).

## IV. INCHOATE CRIMES: Ψ

## A. Solicitation
Solicitation is when a party entices, advises, incites, induces or otherwise encourages another to commit a crime.

Solicitation is complete at the time the solicitation is made. It is unnecessary that the solicited person agree to commit the requested crime. It is also not necessary for the crime to be completed for there to be the crime of solicitation. Impossibility is no defense to solicitation. Additionally, since solicitation is complete at the time of the solicitation, withdrawal is not a defense. Lastly, solicitation merges with the target offense.

**B. Conspiracy**

Conspiracy is a specific intent crime where there is an unlawful agreement between two or more persons with the specific intent to commit the unlawful act. In order for there to be a conspiracy, there must be a meeting of the minds between the parties to act together to accomplish the crime. Some jurisdictions require an overt act in order for there to be a conspiracy. When one conspires with another, each co-conspirator is liable for the crimes of the other conspirator if the crimes are foreseeable and were committed in furtherance of the conspiracy. Conspiracy, unlike solicitation, does not merge with the target offense.

When one co-conspirator is acquitted, the other must also be acquitted because two guilty parties are needed for a conspiracy conviction. Furthermore, under the **Wharton Rule**, there is no conspiracy unless the agreement involves at least two persons. An example is the crime of bigamy, which requires two or more persons to complete the crime.

Impossibility is not a defense to the crime of conspiracy. Additionally, withdrawal is not a defense under the common law. However, in some jurisdictions, withdrawal is a defense if the renouncing party gives timely notice of his withdrawal to all members of the conspiracy and performs an act to prevent the conspiracy.

### C. Attempt

Attempt is where one specifically intends to bring about a crime and pursues a substantial step in furtherance of that intent. The substantial step must bring the defendant significantly close to the completion of the crime. Attempt, like solicitation, merges with the target offense.

Under common law, abandonment was no defense. However, in some jurisdictions, abandonment is a defense if the abandonment was voluntary and complete. Factual impossibility is no defense to attempt but legal impossibility is a defense.

## V. PARTIES TO A CRIME:

### 1. Principal in the First Degree

The principal in the first degree is the actual person who performs the criminal act with the requisite mental state.

### 2. Principal in the Second Degree

A principal in the second degree is the person who is present at the scene of the felony and aids, abets or encourages the commission of the crime with the requisite intent.

### 3. Accomplice Liability

An accomplice is a person who gives assistance or encouragement with the intent to effectuate the commission of a crime. An accomplice is liable for all criminal acts of the principal as long as the crimes were foreseeable. Withdrawal is a defense to accomplice liability when the accomplice repudiates and takes sufficient steps to neutralize the crime.

### 4. Accessory Before the Fact

An accessory before the fact is one who aids, abets, counsels or encourages the commission of a crime but is not present at the scene. An accessory before the fact may be punished to the same extent as the principal and for all crimes within the scope of the conspiracy. Under the common law view, the principal must be convicted for the accessory to be convicted. However, under the modern law, in most jurisdictions, the principal need not be convicted for the accessory to be convicted.

**5. Accessory after the fact**
In order for one to be an accessory after the fact there must be: (1) a completed felony; (2) the accessory must know of the felony; and (3) the accessory must give aid to the felon or hinder the felon's apprehension or conviction.

## VI.    CRIMES AGAINST PERSONS

### A.  Homicide

### 1.  Murder
Murder at common law is defined as the unlawful killing of a human being with malice aforethought. The defendant must be both the legal and factual cause of the killing. The actus reus could be a voluntary act, involuntary act or an omission to act. The mens rea requirement falls into four categories:

**a.   Intentional killing**
An intentional killing arises when the defendant consciously desires with specific intent to kill another person.

**b.   Intentional inflection of serious bodily harm**
Intentional infliction of serious bodily harm murder occurs when the defendant, intending only to cause serious bodily harm, kills another person.

**c.   Depraved heart murder**
Depraved heart murder is the unintentional killing of another person resulting from the

conduct of the defendant which is a reckless wanton indifference to human life.

### d. Felony murder

Felony murder is the intentional killing of another person during the commission or attempted commission of an inherently dangerous felony or before temporary safety is reached after the commission of a felony. Inherently dangerous felonies include: rape, robbery, burglary, arson and kidnapping. In order for a defendant to be convicted of felony murder, the death must be as a consequence of his actions.

Under the **Redline Doctrine**, a felon is not guilty of felony murder where the killing constitutes a justifiable homicide by another such as a police officer or a victim. Additionally, any defense the defendant may raise to the underlying felony is a defense to the felony murder charge.

## 2. Manslaughter Ψ

### a. Voluntary Manslaughter

Voluntary manslaughter is the unintentional killing due to the adequate provocation of another. The adequate provocation element is measured by an objective standard where a reasonable person would also lose self-control. Voluntary manslaughter, also known as a **heat of passion** killing, requires a close time period between the provocation and the killing.

### b. Involuntary Manslaughter

Involuntary manslaughter is the unintentional killing of another person due to criminal negligence or the

commission of an unlawful act <u>without</u> malice
aforethought.

- Criminally negligent involuntary
  manslaughter requires the defendant to
  create a high degree of risk of death or
  serious bodily injury beyond that of ordinary
  negligence.

- Unlawful act involuntary manslaughter is
  the unintentional killing during the
  commission or attempted commission of a
  misdemeanor which is *malum in se* or a
  felony that is not inherently dangerous.

**B. Criminal Battery**
Criminal battery is the unlawful use of force on another that
results in bodily harm or an offensive touching. Criminal
battery is a general intent crime whereby the defendant is
guilty when he acts negligently, recklessly, or the defendant
believes his actions will result in criminal liability.

Aggravated criminal battery is when a defendant causes the
victim serious bodily harm, when the defendant uses a
deadly weapon when committing the battery or when the
defendant batters a woman, child or law enforcement officer.

Defenses to criminal battery include: self-defense, defense of
other, crime prevention and consent.

Criminal battery differs from tortuous battery in that tortuous
battery is a specific intent crime and criminal battery is a
general intent crime. Tortuous battery requires an intention
on the part of the defendant to harm another or cause an
offensive contact. Criminal battery requires reckless,
negligent or an intentional contact.

### C. Criminal Assault

Criminal assault is an attempted battery with the intent to cause physical harm. Aggravated criminal assault, on the other hand, is when the defendant commits an assault with a dangerous weapon or when the defendant acts with the intent to rape or murder another.

### D. Mayhem

Mayhem is when the defendant attempts to maim or do bodily injury by either dismembering the victim or disabling the use of a victim's body part used to defend the victim against the defendant's actions.

### E. Kidnapping

At common law, kidnapping is the unlawful restraint of a person's liberty, by force or by show of force, and the movement of the victim to another county. Most jurisdictions are more liberal in their definition of kidnapping, requiring that the victim only be brought to another location and not another county. Aggravated kidnapping is when the defendant restrains a young child, holds a victim for ransom or kidnaps a victim with the intent to commit a robbery or rape.

### F. Rape

Rape, at common law, is when a male has unlawful sexual intercourse with a female without her consent; even if the parties are married. Statutory rape is when a male has sexual intercourse with a female who is under a certain statutory age set by a particular jurisdiction.

### G. Bigamy

Bigamy is being married to more than one person.

### H. Incest

Incest is when a defendant has sexual relations with a person he or she is closely related to.

**VII.   CRIMES AGAINST PROPERTY**

   **A.  Theft Offenses**

   **1.  Larceny Ψ**

Larceny is the trespassory taking and carrying away of the personal property of another with the intent to deprive the owner of that property permanently. The "carrying away" element is satisfied by the slightest movement of the property. Larceny defines property as any property that is tangible. There cannot be a crime of larceny for abandoned property. However, lost or mislaid property can be the subject of larceny. Larceny is a crime of the possession of another's property. When a person has rightful custody of another's property and misappropriates it, he is usually guilty of embezzlement.

   **2.  Embezzlement Ψ**

Embezzlement is a statutory crime where there is a fraudulent conversion or misappropriation of another's property <u>by one who is in lawful possession of the property</u>.

Embezzlement differs from larceny in that embezzlement requires the defendant to be in lawful <u>possession</u> of the property whereas larceny requires only <u>custody</u> of the property.

   **3.  Robbery**

Robbery requires proof of all the elements of larceny plus two additional elements: (1) the taking must be from the victim's person; and (2) the taking must occur by force, intimidation or threat of violence. <u>Larceny merges with robbery and is, along with assault and battery, a lesser-included offense.</u>

### 4. Obtaining Property by False Pretenses Ψ

A defendant obtains property by false pretenses if the defendant makes a false representation of a material fact that causes the victim to pass title of his property to the defendant who knows the representation to be false.

### 5. Larceny by trick Ψ

Larceny by trick is when the defendant obtains possession of another's property by a representation or a promise that is false at the time he takes possession.

Larceny by trick differs from obtaining property by false pretenses in that <u>larceny by trick requires the defendant to obtain possession, whereas false pretenses requires the defendant to obtain title to the property</u>.

### 6. Receiving Stolen Property

Receiving stolen property is defined as the receiving of property that is <u>known to be stolen</u> with the intent to deprive the owner of it forever.

## B. Crimes Against Habitation

### 1. Burglary

At common law, burglary is defined as the breaking and entering into the dwelling place of another, at night, with the intent to commit a felony or larceny therein.

The "breaking" element of burglary requires an actual or constructive breaking. An actual breaking involves the use of force or by enlarging an existing opening. A constructive entry is achieved by fraud or misrepresentation. Entry is obtained when any part of the defendant's body goes inside the structure.

Most jurisdictions have abolished the "night time" element of burglary and allow a burglary to occur if the crime is committed in the daytime as well. Additionally, jurisdictions have expanded the "dwelling" requirement to include all enclosed structures, not just one's home.

Furthermore, the defendant must intend to commit a felony or larceny <u>at the time of the burglary</u>. If the defendant does not intend to commit a felony or larceny at the time of the breaking and entering, there is no burglary.

2. **Arson**

At common law, arson is defined as the malicious burning of the dwelling place of another. The "burning" element is defined to include even the slightest damage to the "dwelling place" such as <u>charring</u>. However, the mere blackening of a surface is not enough.

CRIMINAL
PROCEDURE

LEGAL PATH
MULTISTATE BAR EXAMINATION
REVIEW

CRIMINAL
PROCEDURE

# CRIMINAL PROCEDURE

## I. FOURTH AMENDMENT: SEARCH AND SEIZURE

### A. The Exclusionary Rule
The exclusionary rule is a constitutional rule used to deter unlawful police conduct. Under this rule, all evidence seized in violation of the 4th Amendment is inadmissible in a criminal proceeding. It does not, however, apply to grand jury proceedings.

### B. Fruits of the Poisonous Tree Doctrine
The fruits of the poisonous tree doctrine states that in addition to excluding evidence which was obtained illegally, any additional evidence obtained either directly or indirectly from the illegal search must also be excluded. Exceptions to the fruits of the poisonous tree doctrine include: (1) evidence that was obtained from an independent source; (2) evidence that would have been discovered eventually regardless of the illegality; and (3) any intervening act of free will of the defendant which purges the otherwise tainted evidence.

### C. Government Conduct Ψ
The 4th Amendment protects persons against governmental conduct and not against searches by private persons. Therefore, any evidence obtained illegally by a private person is admissible in court and not subject to the exclusionary rule. Government conduct includes conduct by law enforcement officials, any persons working at the direction of law enforcement officials, excluding private security guards.

### D. Reasonable Expectation of Privacy Ψ
In order for one to enforce her 4th Amendment rights, there must be a reasonable expectation of privacy. This element is satisfied when the defendant has standing and the objects seized are not held out to the public.

CRIMINAL
PROCEDURE

LEGAL PATH
MULTISTATE BAR EXAMINATION
REVIEW

CRIMINAL
PROCEDURE

A defendant may establish standing to assert a $4^{th}$ Amendment right when his own rights are violated. There is no expectation of privacy where one cannot object to a search. A defendant has automatic standing when: his own property is searched, he lives on the property despite ownership or if he is an overnight guest. However, a passenger in a car who does not own the automobile being searched lacks standing to object to the search.

Items held out to the public do not trigger $4^{th}$ Amendment rights. Examples of items held out to the public include: undeveloped areas outside the curtilage of one's property, discarded property, private conversations where others can hear (with the exception of conversations made in a telephone booth) and luggage sniffed by trained dogs.

E. **Warrant Requirement Ψ**
The $4^{th}$ Amendment requires a warrant for a lawful search, unless there is a recognized exception.

There are four requirements for a warrant to be valid:

**1. Probable Cause**
A valid search warrant must be based on probable cause. Probable cause is where the facts or circumstances are sufficient enough such that a reasonable person would conclude that it is more probable that not that such evidence will be found.

**2. Issued by a Neutral and Detached Magistrate**
Any warrant must be issued by a neutral and detached (unbiased) magistrate after a finding of probable cause for the search warrant.

**3. Supported by Oath or Affirmation**
There must either be oral testimony or an affidavit supporting the facts or circumstances relied upon by the

magistrate. When police officers use hearsay information based on informants, courts use the **Aguilar-Spinelli Test** to determine if there is probable cause. This test requires the police to receive the credible information from a reliable informant. If an informant is determined to be giving credible information and it is reliable, there exists probable cause.

### 4. Particularity
The warrant must describe with specificity the place to be searched and the items to be seized.

The validity of a warrant could be attacked if the defendant could prove by a preponderance of the evidence that the affidavit contained: (1) false statements which were (2) intentional and that (3) a magistrate would not have found there was probable cause if it were not for the false statements.

## F. Exceptions to the Warrant Requirement Ψ
All warrantless searches are unconstitutional unless they fall within a recognized exception. The following are recognized exceptions:

### 1. Search Incident to a Lawful Arrest
A defendant may be searched (as well as the area within his wingspan) without a warrant following a lawful arrest for the officer's protection and to prevent the destruction of evidence. The search must be contemporaneous in time and place of the lawful arrest.

### 2. Stop and Frisk
When a police officer has reasonable suspicion of criminal activity, he may stop and frisk the defendant for concealed weapons.

CRIMINAL
PROCEDURE

LEGAL PATH
MULTISTATE BAR EXAMINATION
REVIEW

CRIMINAL
PROCEDURE

### 3. Automobile Exception
If there is probable cause to search a lawfully stopped automobile, a government official may search any part of the automobile, including containers that may conceal the object of the search. Searches of vehicles may be justified as a search incident to a lawful arrest, plain view or an impounding.

### 4. Plain View
A warrantless search may be justified based on plain view if the government official is lawfully positioned to make the observation of apparent incriminating activity.

### 5. Consent
A search is lawful without a warrant or probable cause if consent is given. For the consent to be valid it must be made intelligently (the defendant must have the capacity to appreciate that which he is consenting to) and made voluntarily. Voluntariness is measured by the totality of the circumstances. The consenting party controls the scope of the consent and any search exceeding that scope is unlawful. Third parties may consent to a search if they have joint control over the property. Any evidence obtained can be used against the other joint occupier.

### 6. Exigent Circumstances
In emergency situations where evidence may be destroyed, a warrantless search may be undertaken.

## II.    FIFTH AMENDMENT

### A. Self-Incrimination
Under *Miranda v. Arizona, 384 U.S. 436 (1966)*, specific warnings must be given to a suspect prior to questioning. The *Miranda* rights are: (1) the defendant has the right to remain silent; (2) anything said by the defendant may be used against him in a court of law; (3) the defendant has the right to an attorney during questioning; (4) if the defendant

cannot afford an attorney one will be appointed for him; and (5) the defendant must understand these rights.

*Miranda* rights attach to a defendant at the time of custodial interrogation. Custodial interrogation is when the defendant is not at liberty to leave and government officials reasonable believe that the defendant will make incriminating statements. However, *Miranda* rights do not attach to spontaneous statements of the defendant without government provocation.

*Miranda* rights need not be repeated after a brief breaking in questioning. If the defendant states a desire to remain silent, all questioning must cease. Additionally, if a defendant requests an attorney during questioning, he invokes his $5^{th}$ Amendment right to counsel as opposed to a $6^{th}$ Amendment right to counsel discussed in the next section.

There are exceptions to *Miranda*, the most important of which is when a government official reasonably believes that the pubic is in danger. In that case, he may question a defendant without giving *Miranda* warnings.

**B. Grand Juries**

States are not constitutionally required to obtain a grand jury indictment before criminally prosecuting a defendant; but in federal court a grand jury indictment is required. Grand juries are used to determine if there is probable cause to prosecute the defendant. If the grand jury does not find probable cause, there can be no criminal prosecution.

If a party is subpoenaed to testify before a grand jury, he is given immunity. The federal courts give witnesses "use immunity." Use immunity precludes the government from using the witness's testimony against him. However, some states use transactional immunity which is broader than use immunity to preclude the use of any independent source evidence against the testifying witness.

CRIMINAL
PROCEDURE

LEGAL PATH
MULTISTATE BAR EXAMINATION
REVIEW

CRIMINAL
PROCEDURE

## C. Double Jeopardy Ψ

The 5th Amendment protects the defendant against double jeopardy. Double jeopardy is where a defendant is tried and punished for the same offense twice. Once a defendant has been tried for an offense, whether convicted or acquitted, double jeopardy attaches and he may not be tried again for the same offense. Furthermore, lesser-included offenses of the same crime may not be tried at a separate trial under double jeopardy. Similarly, merged offenses also cannot be tried separately.

## III. SIXTH AMENDMENT

### A. Right to Counsel

The 6th Amendment states that a defendant shall have the assistance of counsel for his defense. There are ten critical stages of a trial where a defendant enjoys the right to counsel. They are:

1. Custodial interrogation
2. Accusatory stage (arraignment, indictment, arrest)
3. Post charge line-up
4. Post indictment interrogation
5. Preliminary hearings
6. Misdemeanor trials with a chance of imprisonment
7. Felony trials
8. Guilty pleas
9. Sentencing
10. Appeals as a mater of right

### B. Right to a Speedy Trial

The right to a speedy trial attaches when the defendant is arrested or when charges are filed against the defendant. Timeliness is determined by the totality of the circumstances. The factors considered are both the length of the delay and the reason for the delay. If the defendant is the cause of the delay, he losses his right to a speedy trial. On the other hand, if the prosecution is the cause for the delay, absent good cause, the defendant's 6th Amendment rights are violated. The remedy for violating a defendant's 6th Amendment rights is dismissal of the case with prejudice.

## C. Right to an Impartial Jury

The right to an impartial jury attaches for any criminal prosecution for which the potential jail sentence is greater than six months. A defendant may waive his right to a jury trial.

A jury must be composed of at least six persons to satisfy the 6th Amendment. For a six person jury, unanimity is required in federal and state court. In federal court, a twelve person jury requires a unanimous decision to render a verdict, but in state court a 9-3 verdict may be permissible.

The defendant has the right to a jury that is representative of his jurisdiction. During jury selection, each side questions potential jurors for bias. Each side is then given preemptory challenges to disqualify potential jurors for any of a number of reasons (except race). However, a prosecutor may exclude black jurors from the potential jury pool if he can provide a race-neutral reason for doing so (the potential black jurors were excluded for some non-race reason, they just happened to all be black).

## D. Confrontation of Witness

Under the 6th Amendment, a defendant is guaranteed the right to confront any witnesses against him. The purpose of this right is to give the defendant the opportunity to cross-examine persons offering evidence against him and to give the fact finders the opportunity to observe the demeanor of the witness.

CRIMINAL
PROCEDURE

LEGAL PATH
MULTISTATE BAR EXAMINATION
REVIEW

CRIMINAL
PROCEDURE

CONSTITUTIONAL
LAW

LEGAL PATH
MULTISTATE BAR EXAMINATION
REVIEW

CONSTITUTIONAL
LAW

# CONSTITUTIONAL LAW

## I. FEDERAL JUDICIAL POWER

### A. Case or Controversy Requirements

Under Article III, section 2 of the Constitution, the jurisdiction of the federal courts is limited to "cases or controversies" which are real and substantive disputes between parties that can be resolved by a judicial decree.

### 1. Standing Ψ

The Constitution requires that a party arguing a constitutional question must show injury in fact and causation. Injury in fact is proven by a showing by the plaintiff of a direct and personal injury via the action he is complaining about. If, however, the plaintiff has not suffered a harm or injury, then he does not have standing. Causation is proven by the plaintiff showing his harm or injury would not have happened but for the actions of the defendant and the relief sought will redress the injury.

Generally, a plaintiff lacks standing to assert the rights of a third party. However, in certain situations, a party is permitted to raise the constitutional claim of another. If there is a special relationship between the plaintiff and the third party, such as a physician and a patient, the physician could assert the rights of the patient. Where the third party is unable to bring a suit on his own behalf, another may and standing exists. Finally, an association has standing to assert a claim on behalf of its member(s) even if the association has not suffered any injury; providing the member(s) would otherwise have standing on their own, the interest is germane to the association and neither the claim asserted nor the relief sought requires participation by the individual member(s) of the suit.

## 2. Mootness

If the controversy has already been resolved, the case will be dismissed as moot. However, if the parties to a resolved controversy still have an interest, collateral matters to the case will not be dismissed as moot. Additionally, if the injury is capable of repetition, such as a woman who was pregnant when she first challenged the constitutionality of abortion but is no longer pregnant as the suit goes on, the case will not be dismissed as moot (capable of repetition, yet evading review).

## 3. Ripeness

The controversy must also be ripe for decision. Whereas mootness deals with resolved controversies, ripeness deals with claims before they have been fully developed. A case is unripe if there is no real present or future threat of harm.

## 4. Political Question Doctrine Ψ

The court can only review legal questions, not political acts which are within Presidential or Congressional discretion. "Political" does not mean political issues, but issues that are to be decided with finality by one of the other branches of government.

The following are relevant factors which a court must consider in determining if there exists a political question: (1) whether there is a textually demonstrable constitutional commitment of the issue to coordinate a political department; (2) lack of judicially discoverable and manageable standards for resolving it; (3) the impossibility of deciding without an initial policy determination of a kind clearly for non-judicial discretion; (4) the impossibility of the court's undertaking independent resolution without expressing lack of respect to due coordinate branches of government; (5) an unusual need for unquestioning

CONSTITUTIONAL
LAW

LEGAL PATH
MULTISTATE BAR EXAMINATION
REVIEW

CONSTITUTIONAL
LAW

adherence to a political decision already made; or (6) the potentiality of embarrassment from multifarious pronouncements by various departments on one question. *Baker v. Carr, 369 U.S. 186 (1962).*

## B. The United States Supreme Court

According to Article III, section 2 of the Constitution, the Supreme Court has both original and appellant jurisdiction. The Supreme Court has the power to review state court decisions in order to ensure conformity with the Constitution. There are two ways the Supreme Court can review a case; by appeal or writ of certiorari.

With respect to appeals, decisions of three-judge district court panels may be heard by the Supreme Court on appeal. The grounds for certiorari are cases involving conflicts between different federal courts of appeal, cases involving the highest courts of two states, the highest state and federal court on appeal; or cases from state court or U.S. courts of appeal involving important unresolved issues. In order for the Supreme Court to review a case, there must be an independent and adequate state law basis for the decision. This means if there is both a state and federal law issues present and the Supreme Court's reversal of the federal law will not change the result of the case, then the Supreme Court cannot hear the case.

## C. Lower Federal Courts

The 11th Amendment limits a federal court's jurisdiction by not allowing a citizen to sue his resident state or any other state in federal court without that state's consent.

There are exceptions to the 11th Amendment. The 11th Amendment does not preclude suits against state officials for abuse of power in enforcing an unconstitutional state statute. Additionally, the 11th Amendment does not bar the suit of one state by another state or the federal government.

CONSTITUTIONAL
LAW

LEGAL PATH
MULTISTATE BAR EXAMINATION
REVIEW

CONSTITUTIONAL
LAW

Finally, individuals are not precluded from suing state subdivisions such as cities, counties or towns.

## II.    FEDERAL LEGISLATIVE POWER

Article I, section 1 states that all granted legislative power shall be vested in a Congress of the United States. The legislative powers are the powers to make laws, conduct investigations and other things "necessary and proper" to the enactment of legislation.

### A. Taxing Power

The Constitution provides that Congress shall have the power to lay and collect taxes, subject to three limitations:

1. All taxes must be geographically uniform, even if not intrinsically uniform.

2. All direct taxes (taxes imposed directly against property or person responsible for tax burden) must be apportioned among the states.

3. No tax may be laid for goods exported from any state.

Congress may issue taxes for the purposes of regulation as opposed to raising revenue if Congress has the power to tax the activity.

### B. Spending Power

The Constitution provides that Congress may use taxes to pay debts and provide for the common defense and the general welfare of the United States. Congress, by exercising its spending power, may require states to comply with certain conditions in order to qualify for the funds.

### C. Commerce Power

Under Congress' commerce power, Congress can regulate channels, instrumentalities, persons or activities that substantially affect interstate commerce. However, if the

CONSTITUTIONAL
LAW

LEGAL PATH
MULTISTATE BAR EXAMINATION
REVIEW

CONSTITUTIONAL
LAW

activity has no jurisdictional nexus to interstate commerce, Congress has no authority to act.

## III. FEDERAL EXECUTIVE POWER

### A. Foreign Policy

#### 1. Treaties
Under the Supremacy Clause of the Constitution, the President has the power to make treaties with foreign nations and it is effective when ratified by the Senate by a two-thirds vote. Once a treaty is ratified, it is considered to be the supreme law of the land and the judges of every state are bound to respect it unless it conflicts with the Constitution. If a federal law conflicts with a treaty, the one that was enacted last prevails.

#### 2. Executive Agreements
Executive Agreements are agreements made between the President and foreign nations. These agreements prevail over conflicting state laws but never over conflicting federal laws or the Constitution. Additionally, Executive Agreements do not require Senate approval.

### 3. Comparison Chart Ψ

|  | Senate Approval | Conflict of Laws |
| --- | --- | --- |
| Treaties | Yes, 2/3 vote. | Prevail over conflicting state law and federal laws enacted before treaty. |
| Executive Agreements | No Senate approval needed. | Prevail over conflicting state laws but not federal laws or the Constitution. |

#### 4. Commander in Chief
The President has the power to deploy military forces without a formal declaration of war. Although the

CONSTITUTIONAL
LAW

LEGAL PATH
MULTISTATE BAR EXAMINATION
REVIEW

CONSTITUTIONAL
LAW

President could send troops, only the legislature could declare war.

## B. Domestic Affairs

### 1. Appointment Power

The Constitution gives the President the power to appoint Ambassadors, Supreme Court Judges and other officers of the United States. Congress on the other hand may appoint inferior officers to the President, judiciary and heads of departments.

### 2. Removal Power

The President, with no mention in the Constitution, may remove any executive appointee without cause. However, the President must have cause to remove officers performing judicial or quasi-judicial functions.

### 3. Executive Privilege

The President has the absolute privilege to refuse to disclose information (documents, transcripts or conversations) unless an important interest would be served in doing so.

### 4. Pardon Power

Under the Constitution the President has the power to pardon those convicted of federal crimes except for impeachment.

## C. Impeachment of the President

Under the Constitution, the President, Vice President and other officers of the United States may be removed from office on impeachment grounds by being convicted of treason, bribery, or other high crimes and misdemeanors. The House of Representatives, by a two-thirds vote, may impeach but the Senate has the power to try the impeachment.

CONSTITUTIONAL
LAW

LEGAL PATH
MULTISTATE BAR EXAMINATION
REVIEW

CONSTITUTIONAL
LAW

## IV.    FEDERALISM

### A.  Preemption

The Supremacy Clause provides that the Constitution is the supreme law of the land and all treaties made pursuant to it are the supreme law of the land. Therefore, any federal law will supersede any state law that is in direct conflict with it.

Congress can expressly preempt a state law if it states that the federal law is exclusive on that particular state issue. There could also be an implied preemption by Congress. If both the federal law and the state law are exclusive, the federal law preempts the state law. If the state law impedes a federal objective, the federal law preempts the state law. If Congress is clear in its intent to preempt a state law, the federal law preempts the state law.

### B.  The Dormant Commerce

The Commerce Clause gives Congress the power to regulate interstate commerce. The Dormant Commerce Clause allows states to regulate local transactions affecting interstate commerce, if Congress has not enacted legislation on the matter. Under the Dormant Commerce clause, the state regulation must be non-discriminatory and impose no undue burden on interstate commerce.

If the purpose of the state regulation is to discriminate against commerce from another state, the law is invalid. However, if the state is a market participant, the discrimination is allowed. A state, acting as a market participant, may favor its own citizens in receiving benefits from the government or in dealing with a state owned business.

A balancing test is used to determine a non-discriminatory intent. The court will balance the objective and the purpose of the state law against its burden on interstate commerce. If the benefits of the state law outweigh its burden on interstate commerce, then the regulation will be upheld as valid.

CONSTITUTIONAL
LAW

LEGAL PATH
MULTISTATE BAR EXAMINATION
REVIEW

CONSTITUTIONAL
LAW

## V. PRIVILEGES AND IMMUNITIES CLAUSES Ψ

### A. The Privileges and Immunities Clause of the 14th Amendment

The 14th Amendment of the Constitution provides that "No state shall make or enforce any law which shall abridge the privileges and immunities of citizens of the United States." The protection afforded under this clause includes the right to travel interstate, petition Congress, vote for national offices, enter public lands, the right to the protection afforded by U.S. marshals and the right to assemble peacefully. Corporations and aliens are not protected under the 14th Amendment Privileges and Immunities Clause.

### B. The Privileges and Immunities Clause of Article IV, Section 2

The Privileges and Immunities Clause of Article IV, section 2, provides that citizens of each state shall be entitled to the privileges and immunities of citizens in other states. The clause allows for the treatment of in-state persons and out-of-state persons alike with regard to important economic activities or civil liberties unless the out-of-state discrimination it is necessary to achieve an important government purpose.

## VI. CONSTITUTIONAL PROTECTION OF INDIVIDUAL RIGHTS

### A. Government Action

The Constitution only applies to state actions and not private actions. However the 13th Amendment can be used to prohibit private acts of racial discrimination without the requirement of a state action. A state action can be found in the actions of private individuals when the private activity performs a public function or there is state involvement in the private act. A public function is an act that is traditionally performed by the government. State

CONSTITUTIONAL
LAW

LEGAL PATH
MULTISTATE BAR EXAMINATION
REVIEW

CONSTITUTIONAL
LAW

involvement takes place when a state authorizes, encourages or facilitates the unconstitutional activity.

**B. Incorporation of the Bill of Rights**

The Bill of Rights, the first ten amendments of the Constitution, applies directly to the federal government and not the states. However, the 14th Amendment incorporates the Bill of Rights <u>except</u> for the following:

1. The 2nd Amendment right to bear arms.
3. The 3rd Amendment not to have soldiers quartered in one's home.
4. The 5th Amendment right to a grand jury indictment in criminal cases.
5. The 7th Amendment right to a jury trial in civil cases
6. The 8th Amendment right against excessive fines.

**C. Due Process Ψ**

The Due Process Clause, as well as the Equal Protection Clause of the 14th Amendment, protects the rights of persons. Under the two clauses, corporations and aliens are considered persons.

**1. Procedural Due Process**

Procedural Due Process protects the depravation of a person's life, liberty or property without due process of law. A person's life or liberty is deprived when a significant freedom, secured by the Constitution or a statute, is taken away. A personal property interest is deprived when there is a depravation of the continued receipt of a benefit. Once it is determined that a life, liberty or property interest has been deprived, it must be determined what procedures and procedural safeguards the government must afford the individual. To determine this, a balancing test is used which takes into account: (1) the importance of the interest to the individual; (2) the ability of additional procedures to increase the accuracy of the government's fact finding;

CONSTITUTIONAL
LAW

LEGAL PATH
MULTISTATE BAR EXAMINATION
REVIEW

CONSTITUTIONAL
LAW

and (3) the government's interest in administrative efficiency.

## 2. Substantive Due Process

### a. Fundamental Rights
Substantive Due Process was used in the past to invalidate state laws that arbitrarily and unreasonably regulate economic activity. However, today Substantive Due Process is used to regulate an individual's fundamental rights with a level of review known as "strict scrutiny."

Strict scrutiny (discussed later) applies to the fundamental rights. These rights include the right to marry, procreate, obtain custody and raise one's children, keep the family together, use contraception, travel, vote, as well as the 1st Amendment right to free speech, free association and religion.

- **Abortion**
  Abortion does not require strict scrutiny review; rather it requires only an undue burden test. The undue burden test is triggered when a state law puts into effect substantial obstacles to a woman's right to seek an abortion. A woman could choose to have an abortion before the fetus is viable. After a fetus becomes viable, a state may regulate abortions where it is necessary to preserve the health or life of the mother.

  There is no spousal notification or consent requirement before a woman may obtain an abortion. However, parental consent may be required if the woman is under the age of 18,

CONSTITUTIONAL
LAW

LEGAL PATH
MULTISTATE BAR EXAMINATION
REVIEW

CONSTITUTIONAL
LAW

but this requirement could be bypassed by
judicial consent.

**b. The Takings Clause Ψ**

Under the Takings Clause of the 5th Amendment, the
government may take private property for public use
if it pays the owner just compensation. A "taking"
exists where there is government confiscation or the
physical occupation of the property by the
government or its actors. A regulatory "taking"
exists if the government leaves the owner of the land
with no reasonable economically viable use of the
property.

When it is determined that the taking is for public
use or where there is a reasonable belief that the
taking will benefit the public, just compensation
must be paid to the owner. Just compensation is
calculated by paying the owner the market value of
the property.

There is no "taking" if the value of the property has
decreased or if the taking is temporary.
Furthermore, a person may bring an action for a
taking even if the taking existed before he acquired
the property.

## VII. EQUAL PROTECTION

Equal protection violations occur under the 14th Amendment
when persons similarly situated are treated differently. Equal
protection differs from substantive due process in that
substantive due process applies to laws affecting <u>all</u> persons with
respect to the activity, whereas equal protection is triggered
when a law affects only <u>some</u> persons or specific groups with
respect to the activity.

CONSTITUTIONAL
LAW

LEGAL PATH
MULTISTATE BAR EXAMINATION
REVIEW

CONSTITUTIONAL
LAW

## A. Levels of Review Ψ

### 1. Rational Basis Test
Under the rational basis test, a law is upheld if it is rationally related to a legitimate governmental purpose. Under this test, the challenger has the burden of proving no governmental purpose. If the burden is not met, the government usually satisfies the test due to its low threshold. Rational review is used for laws dealing with age, handicap, wealth, alien classifications dealing with self government, and all other classifications not triggered by intermediate or strict scrutiny.

### 2. Intermediate Scrutiny
Under intermediate scrutiny, a law is upheld if it is substantially related to an important governmental purpose. The government always has the burden of persuasion and the government's actual purpose for the law, and not its conceivable purpose, is used in the analysis. Intermediate scrutiny is applied to laws dealing with gender, illegitimacy and undocumented alien children.

### 3. Strict Scrutiny
Under strict scrutiny, a law is upheld if it is necessary to achieve a compelling governmental purpose. The burden of persuasion is always on the government. Under this test, "necessary" is defined as there being no other less restrictive means available to the government to achieve its purpose. Strict scrutiny applies to laws dealing with race, national origin, travel, voting and certain alienage cases.

## B. Discriminatory Classifications
Intentional discrimination, and not a mere discriminatory effect, must be shown in order to trigger intermediate or strict scrutiny. An intentional discriminatory effect could exist on the law's "face" or via the discriminatory intent and the discriminatory impact of the law.

CONSTITUTIONAL
LAW

LEGAL PATH
MULTISTATE BAR EXAMINATION
REVIEW

CONSTITUTIONAL
LAW

## C. Equal Protection Approach

In the analysis, first ask: What is the law's classification? (is there facial discrimination or is there a discriminatory intent?) Next, determine what the level of scrutiny is needed for the discrimination. Last, see if the law meets that level of scrutiny.

## VIII.  THE FIRST AMENDMENT Ψ

### A.  Freedom of Speech

The 1$^{st}$ Amendment of the Constitution provides that Congress shall not abridge the freedom of speech.
The 1$^{st}$ Amendment applies to the states through the 14$^{th}$ Amendment. There are two types of speech regulation: (1) regulation of speech content and (2) regulation of time, place and manner of speech conduct.

### 1.  Regulation of Speech Content

Generally, government regulations aimed directly at the content of the speech or against protected speech, warrant a strict scrutiny standard of review and will be held invalid unless it is necessary to achieve a compelling state interest and narrowly tailored to meet that interest. However, unprotected speech can be regulated if certain requirements are met. The following are unprotected areas of speech (can be regulated by the government):

### a.  Symbolic Speech

Symbolic speech is any communication where the conduct itself is the message to be conveyed. Symbolic speech may be restricted if the regulation (1) furthers an important government interest that is (2) unrelated to the suppression of the speech and (3) alternative channels of communication are left open.

### b.  Defamation

The Constitution could restrict defamatory speech if the plaintiff is a public figure or if the defamatory

CONSTITUTIONAL
LAW

LEGAL PATH
MULTISTATE BAR EXAMINATION
REVIEW

CONSTITUTIONAL
LAW

statement is of a private figure and involves a public concern. In these instances, a plaintiff must prove all the elements of defamation, in addition to proving falsity and fault. In the case of a public figure, the plaintiff must prove actual malice with respect to the defamation. In the case of a private figure, the plaintiff must only prove negligence. The damages for a public figure are compensatory and presumed punitive damages. However, a private figure may be awarded compensatory damages for an actual injury or presumed punitive damages if there is actual malice.

c. **Obscenity**
   Obscene material is unprotected speech and may be regulated if the following conditions are found to exist: (1) the material appeals to the prurient interest in sex of the average community; (2) the material is patently offensive under the law as set by the standard of the community; and (3) the material lacks serious literary, artistic, political or scientific value under a reasonable person standard.

   Obscene material may be regulated by the government through the enactment of zoning ordinances or by the seizure of assets of a business convicted of violating obscenity laws.

   Child pornography is considered unprotected speech and is regulated without satisfying the obscenity test. Private possession of obscene material can not be regulated whereas private possession of child pornography can be regulated by the government.

d. **Commercial Speech**
   Generally, commercial speech is protected under the 1st Amendment. However, false or deceptive advertising can be regulated. In order to determine

CONSTITUTIONAL
LAW

LEGAL PATH
MULTISTATE BAR EXAMINATION
REVIEW

CONSTITUTIONAL
LAW

if commercial speech is lawful, a 3-part test must be
met: (1) the regulation must serve a substantial
interest; (2) the regulation must directly advance the
interest; and (3) the regulation must be narrowly
tailored to serve the substantial interest.

2. **Regulation of Time, Place and Manner of Speech**
Excluding private property, the government may
place reasonable restrictions on the time, place and
manner of speech in public or nonpublic places
(nonpublic places ≠ private property) if specific criteria
are met.

a. **Public and Limited Public Forums**
Any time, place or manner restriction on speech in a
public forum by the governmental must satisfy a
three-part test: The regulation must be: (1) content
neutral as to subject matter and viewpoint (the
regulation must not favor one message over
another); (2) narrowly tailored to serve a significant
governmental purpose; and (3) must leave open
alternative means of communication. Public forums
include streets, sidewalks and parks whereas limited
public forums include libraries and schools.

b. **Nonpublic Forums**
Any time, place; and manner restriction on speech in
nonpublic forums can be regulated if the regulation
is: (1) viewpoint neutral; and
(2) reasonably related to a legitimate governmental
interest. Nonpublic forums include military bases,
airports and jails.

c. **Private Property**
There is no 1$^{st}$ Amendment right to use private
property for speech purposes.

CONSTITUTIONAL
LAW

LEGAL PATH
MULTISTATE BAR EXAMINATION
REVIEW

CONSTITUTIONAL
LAW

## B. Freedom of Association

The 1st Amendment does not explicitly mention the freedom of association. However, the Supreme Court has held that freedom of association derives by implication from the 1st Amendment. Freedom of association prohibits laws that prohibit or punish group memberships. If a law does so, the standard of review is strict scrutiny.

In the case of public employment, an individual cannot be denied employment based upon membership to a political organization unless the potential employee: (1) is an active member of a subversive organization; (2) such membership is with the knowledge of illegal activity; and (3) the potential employee has the specific intent to further those illegal ends.

## C. Freedom of Religion

### 1. The Free Exercise Clause

The Free Exercise Clause prohibits the government from interfering in a person's religious practices or forms of worship as long as the person is sincere in those beliefs; regardless of whether the religion is traditional or nontraditional.

However, conduct in furtherance of one's religious beliefs may be regulated where an individual's conduct is motivated by his religious beliefs and the state has a compelling or important interest in prohibiting the activity. The following are instances where the Free Exercise Clause is overridden by an important or compelling state interest: (1) polygamy, (2) child labor, (3) Sunday closing laws, (4) wearing religious attire, and (5) taxes.

The Free Exercise Clause may not be used to challenge a neutral law of general applicability. For example, the religious use of an illegal drug may not be justified due to the Free Exercise Clause if the prohibition of the drug

CONSTITUTIONAL
LAW

LEGAL PATH
MULTISTATE BAR EXAMINATION
REVIEW

CONSTITUTIONAL
LAW

has nothing to do with the religious belief (e.g., drug use prevention).

## 2. The Establishment Clause

Under the Establishment Clause, the government is prohibited from favoring a particular religion if certain conditions are met. The test for <u>allowing</u> government involvement in such instances is whether: (1) there exists a secular purpose to the government's involvement, (2) the effect of which must neither advance nor inhibit religion, and (3) whether there exists no exclusive entanglement of religion.

For example, it has been held that government sponsored religious activity in public schools is unconstitutional. However, religious groups must have equal access to public school facilities as non-religious groups. It was also held that the government may give aid to religious schools as long as the aid is not used for religious instruction.

## IX. ATTACKING THE CONSTITUTIONALITY OF A STATUTE

### A. Vagueness

A law is unconstitutional on its face if a reasonable person of average intelligence can not logically determine what behavior is being prohibited. A person may challenge a law on its face even though he may not have suffered an injury thereby bypassing the standing requirement.

### B. Overbreadth

A law is unconstitutionally overbroad if it prohibits substantially more conduct than necessary. If the successful challenge to a law is based on overbreadth, the statute is invalidated in its entirety and becomes unenforceable.

CONSTITUTIONAL
LAW

LEGAL PATH
MULTISTATE BAR EXAMINATION
REVIEW

CONSTITUTIONAL
LAW

## C. Prior Restraints

Prior restraints, which are a form of prepublication censorship, are disfavored by the courts. In such instances, the government usually fails to meet its burden of showing that the prior restraint is necessary to prevent direct, immediate or irreparable harm.

# PROPERTY

## I.  PRESENT POSSESSORY ESTATES

An estate is an interest in land that may or may not become possessory.  Land can be owned by more than one person, each with separate and distinct interests, but at any given time only one possessory estate may exist.

### A.  Fee Simple Absolute

An interest in land that is in fee simple absolute is indefeasible.  Indefeasible means that there is an absolute ownership of the entire interest- present and future, without divestment.  In other words, a fee simple absolute is an interest in land that has no restrictions and has a potentially indefinite duration. It can be freely devisable (can pass by will), decendible (can pass by intestacy) and alienable (transferable during the holder's lifetime).

A fee simple absolute interest is created with words such as "to A and his heirs."  However, most states today do not require such precise language to create the interest. Today, a fee simple absolute interest is presumed unless otherwise provided.

Under the Rule in Shelly's Case, if an instrument creates a life estate in A and purports to create a remainder in A's heirs, then the remainder becomes a remainder in fee simple.

### B.  Life Estate

A life estate is an estate that lasts for as long as the possessor lives.  As soon as the possessor dies, the estate either reverts back to the grantor or to a third party.  A life interest is created using the language, "to A for his life," or "for A's life, then to B."  The length of the estate could also be measured by the life of another person.  For example, language such as "to A for the life of B," creates a life estate *per autre vie* (for the life of another).

C. **Fee Tail**

A fee tail is an interest in land that attempts to keep property in a family from generation to generation. However, it is no longer a valid interest today.

A fee tail is created with language such as "to A and the heirs of his body." Today, an attempt to create a fee tail is presumed to create a life estate.

D. **Fee Simple Determinable**

A fee simple determinable is an estate that <u>automatically</u> ends. The grantor has a possibility of reverter upon the stated event. A fee simple determinable estate is devisable, decendible, and alienable.

A fee simple determinable is created with such language as "so long as," "while," and "until." For example, language such as "to A so long as it is used for charity," creates a fee simple determinable estate.

E. **Fee Simple Subject to a Condition Subsequent**

A fee simple subject to a condition subsequent is an interest in land where the grantor has the right to reenter when a certain condition occurs.

A fee simple subject to a condition subsequent is created with language such as "upon condition that," "provided that," and "but if X happens." For example, language such as "to B, but if X occurs back to A," creates a fee simple subject to a condition subsequent.

F. **Fee Simple Subject to an Executory Interest**

A fee simple subject to an executory interest is the same as a fee simple subject to a condition subsequent except that the estate passes to a stated third party instead of to the grantor.

A fee simple subject to an executory interest is created the same way as a fee simple subject to a condition subsequent. For example, language such as "to A, but if X occurs, to C," creates a fee simple subject to an executory interest.

| ESTATE | DEFINITION | CREATION | TRANSFERABILITY | FUTURE INTEREST |
|---|---|---|---|---|
| **Fee Simple Absolute** | An estate with potentially indefinite duration. | To A and his heirs. | Devisable, decendible, and alienable. | None. |
| **Life Estate** | An estate in a person until he dies. | To A for life or to A for the life of B (per autre vie). | | Reversion back to the grantor or his heirs. |
| **Fee Simple Determinable** | Estate that automatically reverts back to the grantor upon a stated event. | To A and his heirs, so long as the property is used for X. | Devisable, decendible, and alienable. | Possibility of reverter to grantor. |
| **Fee Simple Subject to a Condition Subsequent** | Grantor could retake estate upon a stated event. | To A, but if X occurs, then to grantor. | Back to grantor if condition occurs. | Right of reentry. |
| **Fee Simple Subject to an Executory Interest** | If stated condition occurs, interest goes to 3rd party. | To A, but if X occurs, to B. | To 3rd party if event occurs. | Shifting or springing executory interest discussed later. |
| **Fee Tail** | Estate goes to the decendent of a particular person. | To A and the heirs of his body. | Creation of a fee tail created a fee simple absolute instead. | Reversion to the grantor or Remainder if it goes to a 3rd party. |

## II. FUTURE INTERESTS

### A. Future Interests in Grantor
A future interest in a grantor is a reversionary interest. There are three types of reversionary interests:

1. **Reversion**
   A reversion is an automatic transfer of an interest in property back to the grantor. This arises when the estate in a grantee terminates in a manner other than by a condition.

   Under the **Doctrine of Worthier Title**, if a grantor attempted to convey property with a future interest in the grantor's heirs, the future interest is void and the heirs get nothing while the grantor retains a reversion.

2. **Possibility of Reverter**
   A possibility of reverter always deals with a fee simple determinable estate. A possibility of reverter exists if there is a condition on the use of the property. A possibility of reverter differs from a reversion in that a reversion is certain to occur whereas a possibility of reverter may never happen.

3. **Right of Reentry**
   A right of reentry arises when a condition is broken and is seen in conjunction with a fee simple subject to a condition subsequent.

B. **Future Interests in Third Parties**

1. **Remainder Interests**
   A remainder occurs when a future interest in a third party expires.

   a. **Vested Remainder**
      A vested remainder is a remainder created in ascertained (known) persons and not subject to a condition subsequent. There are three types of vested remainders:

- **Indefeasible Vested Remainder**
  An indefeasible vested remainder is a future interest <u>certain</u> to become possessory.

- **Vested Remainder Subject to Total Divestment**
  A vested remainder subject to total divestment is a future interest which must vest if a prior possessory interest terminates in time.

- **Vested Remainder Subject to Open**
  A vested remainder subject to open is a future interest which is certain to vest in someone but there is a chance that persons that are not ascertainable may also take and share in the estate.

b.  **Contingent Remainder**
    A contingent remainder is an estate created in unascertained persons and or subject to a condition precedent.

c.  **Executory Interest**
    An executory interest is a future interest created in a third party that is not a remainder. There are two types of executory interests:

    - **Shifting Executory Interest**
      A shifting executory interest cuts short another's interest who is not the grantor. For example, "To A and his heirs, but if B returns within a year, to B and his heirs," is a shifting executory interest.

    - **Springing Executory Interest**
      A springing executory interest divests the transferor in the future. For example, "To A

when he marries B," is a springing
executory interest.

| Future Interest | Vested Remainder | Contingent Remainder | Executory Interest |
|---|---|---|---|
| **Definition** | Future interest created in ascertained persons not subject to condition precedents. | Future interest created in unascertained persons and or subject to a condition precedent. | Future interest created in 3$^{rd}$ parties which is not a remainder. |
| **Variation of the Future Interest** | • Indefeasible Vested Remainder <br>• Vested Remainder Subject to Total Divestment | | • Shifting Executory Interest <br>• Springing Executory Interest |

## C. The Rule against Perpetuities

The rule against perpetuities states that a future interest is void if there is any possibility that the interest will not vest within 21 years of some life in being at the creation of the interest.

The elements of the rule against perpetuities are:

### 1. Vesting

A vested remainder subject to open vests when the class closes. A contingent remainder vests when the grantee is ascertainable and there are no condition precedents. An executory interest vests when the parties receive possession. It is not necessary that the interest actually vest but that the vesting does not occur to far in the future. Some states implement the **Wait and See Doctrine**, which states that contingent remainders are not automatically void, but are allowed if they vest within the rule.

### 2. Twenty-one Year Rule
Conveyance of an interest may not occur more than 21 years after a life in being.

### 3. Life in Being
A life in being does not have to be the grantor's life, but can be anyone connected to the interest.

### 4. At the Creation of the Interest
This means that the rule against perpetuities is triggered when the creating instrument takes effect.

## III. CONCURRENT ESTATES Ψ
There are three major concurrent estates: joint tenancy, tenancy in common, and tenancy by the entirety.

### A. Joint Tenancy
A joint tenancy is a form of co-ownership in which the tenant owners own an undivided interest in the whole estate. Each joint tenant has the right to possess the whole estate. The most significant factor of a joint tenancy is when one of the joint tenants dies; the remaining interest automatically goes to the surviving tenants. A joint tenancy interest <u>cannot</u> be passed to heirs. Additionally, there is no severance of the joint tenancy with the execution of a mortgage, a lease, a lien or divorce decree.

A joint tenancy is created with the <u>four utilities</u> of: time, title, interest and possession. If even one of the unities is lacking, the joint tenancy fails and a tenancy in common is created. Unity of time requires that all of the tenants' interests in the property vest at the same time. Unity of title requires the interest to be acquired by the same instrument. Unity of interest requires the tenants to share the exact same interest in the property (e.g., duration). Also, all of the tenants must have a right to occupy the entire estate.

Although traditional law presumes a transfer of property to A and B is a joint tenancy, joint tenancy estates are not preferred by the courts today. Therefore, express words are needed to create such an interest. For example, words such as "To A and B as joint tenants with the right of survivorship" or "To A and B as joint tenants," create a joint tenancy.

A joint tenancy can be terminated by a sale, partition or a mortgage of the property. With respect to mortgaging the property, under a **lien theory,** a mortgage by one tenant on the property does not sever the tenancy. However in a **title theory** jurisdiction, a mortgage by one tenant does sever the tenancy.

**B. Tenancy in Common**
A tenancy in common is a concurrent ownership where each tenant owns a separate share of the property but has an equal right to possess the whole regardless of the actual share owned. This type of ownership has no right of survivorship and each tenant may pass his interest in the property (e.g., the property is freely alienable).

A tenancy in common is created by default. However, a tenancy in common is terminated by the ouster of a tenant, merger of tenant's interests, death of a tenant or partition of the property.

**C. Tenancy by the Entirety**
A tenancy by the entirety is a co-ownership of property similar to a joint tenancy but solely based on husband and wife ownership. A tenancy by the entirety is created using the same four utilities for a joint tenancy (time, title, interest and possession), with the additional utility of a valid marriage between husband and wife. A tenancy by the entirety can be terminated by a transfer of the property, death of a spouse or divorce. If both husband and wife intend to transfer the interest, then the transfer is valid. If only one

spouse attempts to terminate the interest, the termination will be held invalid. The death of a spouse turns the interest in the property into a fee simple in the surviving spouse. A valid divorce decree severs a tenancy by the entirety, creating a joint tenancy in one person or a tenancy in common.

| ESTATE | DEFINATION | CREATION | TERMINATION |
|---|---|---|---|
| **Joint Tenancy** | Tenancy acquired by two or more persons with the right of survivorship. | Four Utilities:<br>• Time<br>• Title<br>• Interest<br>• Possession | • Sale<br>• Partition<br>• Mortgage |
| **Tenancy in Common** | Property owned concurrently by two or more persons with a right to possess the whole with no right of survivorship. | Default tenancy. | • Ouster<br>• Merger<br>• Death<br>• Partition |
| **Tenancy by the Entirety** | Property held between husband and wife. | Four utilities and a valid marriage. | • Transfer<br>• Death<br>• Divorce |

IV.    **NON-FREEHOLD ESTATES**

A.  **Estate for Years**
An estate for years is an interest in property that lasts for a fixed period of time as set fourth in a lease. An estate for years is terminated automatically at the expiration of the lease or upon surrender by the leaseholder.

B.  **Periodic Tenancy**
A periodic tenancy is a tenancy for a fixed duration and continues for succeeding periods until either the landlord or

the tenant gives notice of termination. If no notice is given, then the tenancy extends for another duration period.

A periodic tenancy is created by the express agreement of both parties, by implication or by operation of law. A periodic tenancy is created by implication if a lease provides for no termination date but there exist consistent payments of rent in fixed duration periods (monthly rent). A periodic tenancy is created by operation of law where the tenant holds over after the expiration of the lease term (discussed below).

A periodic tenancy is terminated with proper notice. Notice can be given orally or by writing. The notice must equal the length of the rental period except in the instance of an annual lease (only 6 months notice is required). For example, if a lease term creates week to week tenancy, notice must be given one week prior to termination.

## C. Tenancy at Will
A tenancy at will is a tenancy with no stated duration, either by express terms or by operation of law. A tenancy at will continues as long as both the landlord and tenant agree to continue. If either the landlord or tenant wishes to terminate the tenancy, the tenancy is terminated. Notice is not required to terminate a tenancy at will.

## D. Holdover Tenant
A holdover tenant is a tenant that continues in possession after the termination of the tenancy. Once a tenant becomes a holdover tenant, the landlord has two options: (1) allow the tenant to stay on the premises or (2) evict him. Most jurisdictions allow for a periodic tenancy to be created once the landlord consents to the tenant staying on the premises. The new period is measured by the length of the original tenancy duration and governed by the provisions of the old lease.

| ESTATE | DEFINATION | CREATION | TERMINATION |
|--------|-----------|----------|-------------|
| **Estate for Years** | Tenancy for a fixed period of time. | Written lease. | • Expiration of lease<br>• Surrender of lease holder |
| **Periodic Tenancy** | Tenancy for durational intervals. | • Expressly<br>• Implication<br>• Operation of law | • Proper notice |
| **Tenancy at Will** | Tenancy with no stated duration. | • Express terms<br>• Operation of law | • By either landlord or tenant. |
| **Holdover Tenant** | When a tenant holds over after the termination of the tenancy. | When tenant stays past allowed duration of possession. | • Creation of a periodic tenancy<br>• Eviction |

## V. LANDLORD AND TENANT DUTIES

### A. Landlord Duties

#### 1. Duty to Deliver Possession
Under the common law, a landlord impliedly warrants that the tenant will have a legal right to possess of the premises. However, under the modern view, a landlord does not have an obligation to deliver possession of the premises.

#### 2. Quiet Enjoyment
Every lease has an implied covenant of quiet enjoyment. An eviction of a tenant by a landlord breaches this covenant. There are two types of evictions, actual and constructive. Actual eviction occurs when the landlord excludes the tenant from the leased premises. Constructive eviction arises from the negligent conduct

of the landlord that makes the leased premises uninhabitable.

### 3. Suitable Premises
A landlord is not liable for dangerous conditions existing on the leased premises. However, he may be liable in tort to the tenant, his guests, licensees, or invitees if, at the commencement of the lease, there existed a latent defect (dangerous condition) the landlord knew of or should have known about and it was not likely to be discovered by the tenant upon her reasonable inspection.

### 4. Duty to Repair
Under common law, absent a statute to the contrary, the landlord has no duty to maintain the leased premises. However, if the landlord does undertake a repair on the premises and does so negligently he is liable in tort for any injuries.

## B. Tenant Duties

### 1. Duty to Pay Rent
A tenant has the duty to pay rent to the landlord for the leased premises.

### 2. Duty to Repair
A tenant has a duty to make ordinary repairs and maintain the leased premises.

### 3. Duty not to commit Waste
A tenant may not commit ameliorative waste on the leased premises. Ameliorative waste is changing the physical characteristics of the premises. This includes improvements to the leased premises which increase the value of the land/premises.

## C. Fixtures

A fixture is a chattel that becomes real property because it has been permanently attached to the leased premises and may not be removed by the tenant. However, if the fixture is a trade fixture, it is removable by the tenant. A trade fixture is a fixture installed for a particular business purpose. Modern law, on the other hand, allows for all fixtures to be removed as long as the premises can be returned to its former condition.

## D. Assignments and Subleases

### 1. Assignments

An assignment occurs when a tenant transfers the entire term of a lease and retains no interest in the lease. The original tenant is no longer in privity of estate but remains in privity of contract with the landlord. Therefore, if the assignee fails to pay his rent, the landlord may recover against the original tenant. However, if the assignee assumes all the promises in the original lease, there is privity of contract between the landlord and assignee, and the original tenant is not liable for any non-payment of rent.

> - T1 (Original Tenant) transfers whole lease to T2 (Second Tenant).
>
> - L (Landlord) and T2 are in privity of estate and liable to each other.
>
> - L and T2 are NOT in privity of contract unless T2 expressly assumes all promises of the original lease.

### 2. Subleases
A sublease occurs when a tenant transfers <u>less than</u> the entire leasehold. The tenant remains in both privity of estate and privity of contract with the landlord. In this situation, the sublessee has created no legal relationship between the landlord and himself and is therefore not liable to pay rent to the landlord.

---

- T1 (Original Tenant) transfers part of the lease to T2 (Sublessee).

- L and T2 share no nexus and are not in privity of estate or contract.

---

### 3. Covenants against Assignments or Subleases
Some leases contain provisions that forbid assignments or subleases without the consent of the landlord. Such provisions are strictly construed against the landlord and are usually invalid.

## VI. EASEMENTS
An easement is the right of a person to go onto the land of another to make limited use of the property.

### A. Easement Classifications

### 1. Easement Appurtenant
An easement appurtenant is an easement created to benefit another tract of land, the use of which is incident to the ownership of the land. There are two parcels of land that are involved in an easement appurtenant; the dominant estate and servient estate. The dominant estate is the land whose owner is benefited by the easement. The servient estate is the land that is burdened by the easement.

### 2. Easement in Gross

An easement is gross is an easement benefiting a particular person and not a particular piece of land. For example, A's use of a billboard on B's land is an easement in gross because the billboard is benefiting A and not B's land.

### 3. Affirmative Easements

An affirmative easement is an easement that forces the owner of the servient estate to permit certain actions by the easement holder. For example, if A is permitted to discharge water onto B's servient estate, there is an affirmative easement.

### 4. Negative Easements

A negative easement is an easement that prohibits the owner of the servient estate from doing something. For example, if A is prohibited from building a structure that obstructs the view of B's building, a negative easement is present.

## B. Creating an Easement Ψ

### 1. Creation by Express Grant

Easements are subject to the statute of frauds and therefore must be in writing and signed by the party charged. If, however, the easement is not in writing but is oral, a license is created and not an easement. However, an easement in favor of the conveyer that is appurtenant to the tract retained is called a reservation.

### 2. Creation by Implication

An easement by implication is created by operation of law and is an exception to the statute of frauds. In order for there to be a valid easement by implication, four requirements must be met: (1) at the time of the conveyance, one part of the land is being used for the benefit of the other part; (2) the use is apparent; (3) the use is continuous; and (4) the use is either reasonably or strictly necessary to the enjoyment of the dominant tract.

### 3. Creation by Necessity
An easement by necessity is created if the owner of a tract of land divides the tract into two lots and deprives one lot access to a public road.

### 4. Creation by Prescription
An easement by prescription is created by an adverse use of the servient estate by the dominant estate. An easement by prescription requires: (1) adverse use; (2) continuous use for the statutory period of time; (3) open and notorious use; and (4) no interruption.

## C. Terminating an Easement

### 1. Estoppel
An easement is terminated by estoppel when the servient estate reasonably relies on the conduct of the owner of the dominant estate and uses his servient estate in a manner inconsistent with the existence of the easement and it would be inequitable to use the easement further.

### 2. The Necessity is Over
Once the necessity is over, the easement that was created due to the necessity is terminated.

### 3. Destruction of the Property
If the easement is a structure and it is involuntarily destroyed, the easement is terminated.

### 4. Condemnation
Condemnation of the servient estate will terminate the easement. However, most jurisdictions allow compensation for any lost value.

5. **Abandonment Ψ**

If the dominant tenant intends to abandon the use of the easement, the easement is terminated. However, non-use of an easement <u>does not</u> terminate an easement. If there is non-use of the easement <u>and</u> an intent to abandon the easement, the easement is terminated.

6. **Merger**

When both the dominant and serviant estates merge into a single possession by another person, any easements present are terminated.

D. **Licenses Ψ**

A license is a permit for one to come onto the land possessed by another without being considered a trespasser. A license is a privilege and therefore can be revoked at the will of the licensor <u>unless</u> it is coupled with an interest.

## VII. COVENANTS AT LAW AND EQUITABLE SERVITUDES

Covenants at law serve to bind future owners of land who are not parties to the original contract by enforcing promises against successors in interest of the original parties. At law, such promises are enforced as covenants at law and in equity as equitable servitudes. Covenants at law could be affirmative or negative. Affirmative covenants are promises to do something, whereas negative covenants are promises not to do something.

A. **Common Elements Between Covenants at Law and Equitable Servitudes**

1. **Touch and Concern the Land**

Both covenants at law and equitable servitudes must touch and concern the land. This means that both the benefits and burdens placed on the land must pass to succeeding landholders.

2. **Intent to Run With the Land**

Both covenants at law and equitable servitudes must be intended by the covenantor and covenantee to "run with the land." This is accomplished by language which clearly states the intent of the promise to "run with the land."

### 3. Writing
In order for there to be a valid covenant at law or equitable servitude, there must be a writing to satisfy the statute of frauds. However, in the case of **negative equitable servitudes,** where a developer divides land and some deeds contain negative covenants and some do not, the negative covenants will be binding on all parcels of land even without a writing if there is a common scheme of development and the owner had notice.

## B. Additional Elements for Covenants at Law

### 1. Privity

#### a. Vertical Privity
Vertical privity is a relationship between successors in interest involving covenanting parties. For example, if A transfers to B, and B transfers to C, A and C are in vertical privity.

#### b. Horizontal Privity
Horizontal privity is a relationship involving a common grantor. For example, if A sells a plot of land to B, and B sells the plot to C; then A, B and C are in horizontal privity.

### 2. Damages
The remedy for a breach of a covenant at law is damages.

## C. Additional Elements for Equitable Servitudes

### 1. Notice
Notice could be actual, constructive or inquiry and must be in writing.

## 2. Damages
The remedy for a breach of an equitable servitude is an injunction.

## VIII.   ADVERSE POSSESSION Ψ
Adverse possession is a method of acquiring title to property by possession for a statutory period of time if certain elements are met. The elements of adverse possession are:

### A.   Hostile
The adverse possessor must be hostile in his possession of the land. This means that the adverse possessor must not have the permission of the true owner to use the land.

### B.   Actual
The possession of the land by the adverse possessor must be consistent with the normal use of the land. For example, if the land is used seasonally, seasonal use of the land by the adverse possessor satisfies the element.

### C.   Open and Notorious
The open and notorious element is satisfied when the adverse possessor puts the true owner on notice that a trespass is occurring on the true owner's land.

### D.   Exclusive
The adverse possessor is not sharing the land with the true owner or the public.

### E.   Continuous for the Statutory Period of Time
Each jurisdiction has a statutory period of time for which an adverse possessor must occupy the land of the true owner for the element to be satisfied. At common law, the statutory period of time is twenty years. However, there need not be continuous possession by the same person. The period of adverse possession of one possessor could be "tacked" to the period of adverse possession of another possessor when there is privity between the two.

## IX.    CONVEYANCE OF TITLE OF REAL PROPERTY

### A.  The Deed
A deed is a written instrument by which land is conveyed.

#### 1.  The Elements of a Deed
The statute of frauds requires that contracts for the sale of land be in writing and signed by the grantor. However, under the **Part Performance Doctrine** (discussed later) an oral contract for the sale of land may be specifically enforced if certain conditions are met. The elements of a deed are as follows:

a.  Signature of the grantor
b.  Consideration
c.  Identification of the buyer and seller
d.  Description of the property
e.  Grantor's intent to delivery the deed
f.  Acceptance of the deed by grantee

#### 2.  Types of Deeds

##### a.  Warranty Deed
A warranty deed is a deed that expressly guarantees the grantor's good clear title and contains covenants concerning the quality of tile including:

- **Warrantees of Seisin** - grantor owns the property he purports to convey.
- **Quiet Enjoyment** - grantee will not be disturbed in his possession of the property.
- **Right to Convey** - grantor has the right to convey the property he purports to convey.
- **Freedom of Encumbrances** - the property is free from any liens.
- **Defense of Title Against all Claims** - the grantor will perform whatever acts may be

reasonably necessary to protect the grantee's title.

### b. Special Warranty Deed
A special warranty deed is a deed in which the grantor covenants to warrant and defend the title against claims and demands of only the grantor and all persons claiming by and under him.

### c. Quitclaim Deed
A quitclaim deed is a deed that conveys a grantor's complete interest or claim in real property but neither warrants nor professes that the title is valid.

## B. Part Performance
Under the part performance doctrine, an oral contract to sell land is enforceable in equity despite the statute of frauds (requirement of a writing). Part performance can come in many forms. However, the acts that are recognized by the courts for part performance are the following:

Payment of all or part of the purchase price, and either:

a. delivery of possession of the land to the vendee; or
b. via the construction of permanent and valuable improvements by the vendee.

## C. Equitable Conversion
Equitable conversion is the doctrine that treats interests in land as if they have already been converted into personal property. This doctrine states that the purchaser is the equitable owner of the land and not the vendor, even though he may still have legal title to the land. Therefore, if a piece of property is destroyed during the executory period (time between when the contract is signed and the closing) but before the closing, and neither party is at fault, the risk of loss is on the buyer and he must pay the contract price.

However, a minority of states follow the **Uniform Vendor and Purchaser Risk Act** (UVPRA). Under this Act, the risk of loss is on the seller during the executory period unless the buyer has actually taken possession of the property or has legal title to the property at the time the property is destroyed.

**D. Marketable Title**
Land contracts come with an implied assurance of marketable title. If, however, the vendor fails to deliver marketable title, the vendee may rescind the contract.

The vendor is only obligated to tender marketable title on the closing date and the purchaser may not rescind the contract before the time of performance. If the buyer becomes aware that that the title is unmarketable, he must notify the seller and allow him (the seller) reasonable time to cure the defect even if it extends past the closing date. If the seller fails to cure the defect within a reasonable time, the buyer may rescind the contract. The buyer may also sue for damages for the breach or specific performance including a reduction in the purchase price to reflect the defect in title.

The following are defects that render title unmarketable: Ψ

1. Encumbrances
2. Encroachments
3. Easements
4. Mortgages or liens
5. Restrictive Covenants
6. Land subject to claims of adverse possession

**E. Recording Statutes Ψ**
Recording statutes provide a means of giving constructive notice of ownership of a piece of property by recording them with the county clerk's office. Recording statutes apply to deeds as well as mortgages and are only applicable when two parties each claim to be the record titleholder of a

particular piece of property. There are three types of recording statutes depending on the jurisdiction:

**1. Race Statutes**

Under this statute the first party to record holds the title to the piece of property.

**2. Notice Statutes**

Under this statute, the last bona fide purchaser of the property for value has title to the piece of property. A bona fide purchaser for value is a person who tenders value for property and is without notice that there is a previous buyer of the same piece of property.

**3. Race Notice Statutes**

Under this statute, the first bona fide purchaser for value who records has title to the piece of property.

## X. LAND USE

### A. Zoning

A state, through its enabling act, has zoning powers. All zoning ordinances must be authorized by the state's legislature and will be held valid unless they are arbitrary and unreasonable, having no substantial relation to the public health, safety, morals or general welfare. Additionally, zoning ordinances must be enacted with notice or there will be a violation of due process and thus the ordinance will be held unconstitutional.

### B. Support Ψ

All landowners must maintain support for the benefit of adjacent lands. If an excavator is negligent in causing improved land to cave in, he is liable for any damages. Strict liability attaches to an excavator if his actions would have caused the cave in of the property in its natural state.

## C. Waste
Waste is a commission or omission by one in possession of land. There are three types of waste on land:

### 1. Voluntary Waste
Voluntary waste is an affirmative, willful action by one in possession of land via the stripping its value.

### 2. Permissive Waste
Permissive waste is committed by the omitted actions of a possessor of the land.

### 3. Ameliorative Waste
Ameliorative waste is when one in possession of land actually enhances its value.

## D. Water Rights Ψ

### 1. Allocation of Water in Watercourses
There are two major theories for the allocation of water in watercourses. Eastern states follow the Riparian Water Right Doctrine, whereas western states follow the Prior Appropriation Doctrine.

#### a. Riparian Water Rights
Under this doctrine, water in watercourses belongs to those who own the land bordering the watercourse and the water can only be used in connection with that parcel. There are two theories for riparian rights, the Reasonable Use Theory and the Natural Flow Theory.

- **Reasonable Use Theory**
  Under the Reasonable Use Theory, a riparian owner is subject to liability for making unreasonable use of the water in a watercourse that causes harm to another riparian owner's reasonable use of the water. There are several factors that are used to determine the

reasonableness of the use of the water. They are: purpose of the use, where the water is being taken from and the extent of the use.

- **Natural Flow Theory**
  Under this theory, a riparian owner is entitled to the use of adjacent watercourses in their natural condition.

b. **Prior Appropriation Doctrine**
   Under this minority theory, priority is determined by the first person to arrive and use the watercourse.

2. **Underground Water**
   There are three different rules for determining underground water rights: reasonable use, absolute ownership and appropriation rights.

a. **Reasonable Use Doctrine**
   The Reasonable Use Doctrine is the majority view. Under this doctrine, a proprietor of land may withdrawal underground water for a beneficial purpose and is not subject to liability for interference with the use of another's water use unless: (1) the withdrawal of water causes harm to a neighbor; (2) the withdrawal of water is not for a reasonable use; or (3) the withdrawal has a direct effect on the watercourse.

b. **Absolute Ownership Doctrine**
   An owner of land can take as much water from under his property as he wishes for any purpose.

c. **Appropriate Rights Doctrine**
   Under this doctrine, the first to use the water has the priority right.

### 3. Surface Water

An owner of land may use surface water that is within his boundary line for any purpose. There are three theories for the use of surface water:

#### a. Common Enemy Theory

Under this theory, an owner of property may take protective measures to get rid of surface water.

#### b. Natural Flow Theory

Under this theory, owners of property cannot alter natural drainage patterns.

#### c. Reasonable Use Theory

Under this theory, a balancing test is used to determine the reasonableness of the use of the surface water. Specifically, the utility of the use is balanced against the harm caused.

### E. Eminent Domain

Eminent domain allows the federal and state governments to take title to private property against the owner's will. However, the taking must be for public use and reasonable compensation must be paid to the owner for the property.

## XI. MORTGAGES

A mortgage is an interest in land created in an instrument providing security for the performance of a duty or the payment of a debt. The mortgage must be signed and in writing to satisfy the statute of frauds. The parties to a mortgage are the mortgagor (who is the debtor) and the mortgagee (who is the lender, e.g., a bank). If the mortgagor does not pay the mortgage debt on time, the mortgagee may claim title to the property or sell the property and keep the proceeds to satisfy the debt. Any obligation capable of being reduced to its monetary equivalent may be secured by a mortgage.

## A. TYPES OF MORTGAGES

### 1. Purchase Money Mortgage
A purchase money mortgage is a mortgage that a buyer gives the seller when the property is conveyed to secure the unpaid balance of the purchase price.

### 2. Equitable Mortgage
An equitable mortgage is a mortgage where property is posted as security for a loan and the deed is transferred to a creditor to be reconvened if the debt is not paid.

### 3. Recourse Mortgage
This is a mortgage where the mortgagor is personally liable to the mortgagee for any deficiency in the event of a foreclosure.

### 4. Non-recourse Mortgage
This is a mortgage where the mortgagor is not personally liable to the mortgagee for any deficiency in the event of a foreclosure.

## B. Taking Property Subject to the Mortgage or Assuming the Mortgage

If a seller conveys property to the buyer without satisfying the mortgage, the grantee will take the property either subject to the mortgage or by assuming the mortgage.

### 1. Subject to the Mortgage
When a buyer takes property subject to the mortgage, the buyer is not personally liable for the mortgage debt. If the mortgage is not paid, the mortgagee may foreclose on the property.

### 2. Assuming the Mortgage
When a buyer takes property and assumes the mortgage of the seller, he is personally liable for the debt. The mortgagee may therefore hold either the buyer or the

seller liable for the full debt. If, however, the mortgagee holds the seller liable, the buyer will be liable to the seller since he assumed the debt.

## C. Termination of the Mortgage
A mortgage may be terminated by the following:

### 1. Payment
If the debt is paid in full, the mortgage is satisfied and the mortgage note is terminated.

### 2. Merger
If the mortgagor and the mortgagee merge their interests, the mortgage is terminated.

### 3. Foreclosure
Foreclosure is an equitable remedy when the mortgagor defaults on the mortgage. This is one option a mortgagee may use to recover any and all money lent to the mortgagor to purchase the property. In a foreclosure, the property is sold and the proceeds are used to satisfy the debt. If the proceeds are insufficient to satisfy the debt, the mortgagee may bring a personal action against the mortgagor for the deficiency.

If the mortgagor defaults on a mortgage payment, a majority of jurisdictions allow for a redemption of the property. However, a minority of jurisdictions do not. The right of redemption allows the mortgagor the opportunity to pay off the mortgage and keep the property. There are two types of redemption:

#### a. Redemption in Equity
Redemption in equity allows the mortgagor to redeem the mortgaged property if he pays off the entire mortgage before the foreclosure sale.

**b. Statutory Redemption**
Statutory redemption allows the mortgagor to
redeem the mortgaged property if the mortgage is
paid in full within the statutory period of time,
which could range from six months to one year.

If there are multiple mortgages on a piece of property,
the first mortgage is called the senior mortgage and all
subsequent mortgages are called junior mortgages. In
the event of a foreclosure initiated by the senior
mortgagor, only junior mortgages that are named in the
foreclosure may collect to satisfy their debt. If a junior
mortgage is not named in the foreclosure action, it must
wait until other debts are paid before its debt can be
satisfied.

# INDEX

## A

# M

# P

## S